Hidden Grace

Growing Through Loss and Grief

WILLIAM L. BLEVINS

FirstXaris Books

Hidden Grace: Growing Through Loss and Grief
ISBN: Softcover 978-1-960326-86-7
Copyright © 2024 by William L. Blevins

FirstXaris Books is an imprint of Parson's Porch & Company (PP&C) in Cleveland, Tennessee. PP&C is a self-funded charity which earns money by publishing books of noted authors, representing all genres. Its face and voice is **David Russell Tullock** who you can contact at: dtullock@parsonsporch.com.

Parson's Porch & Company *turns books into bread & milk* by sharing its profits with the poor.

www.parsonsporch.com

Hidden Grace

Contents

In Memory of Kym

And her nieces and nephews Alex, Jaclyn, Sydney, Noah, and Neal

Foreword

Preface

The confrontation with death- and the reprieve from it- makes everything look so precious, so sacred, so beautiful that I feel more strongly than ever the impulse to love it, to embrace it, and to let myself be overwhelmed by it. My river never looked so beautiful....

Death and its ever-present possibility makes love, passionate love, more possible. I wonder if we could love passionately, if ecstasy would be possible at all, if we knew we'd never die.

--Abraham Maslow, in a letter while he recuperating from a heart attack

Carolyn was a very conscientious student. That's why I was curious about her absence from class. And that's why, a few days later, I stopped her in the hallway outside my office. Our conversation was brief and went something like this:

"Hi, Carolyn. I missed you in class last week."

"Thanks. My grandfather died and I attended his funeral."

"I'm very sorry. Was his death unexpected?"

"Not really. His health had been declining/ or some time. We knew he didn't have long to live. But it was still a shock ... you know, it's just hard to say goodbye."

"It's hard to say goodbye!" I knew immediately what Carolyn meant. For at that time my father was slowly dying of cancer. He had been suffering with this disease for over three years. During that time, we talked on several occasions about his impending death. Such talk was difficult for both of us. Yet the process of saying goodbye as he died was just as natural as saying hello when I was born.

Our effort to say goodbye was not always vocal. I remember one particular day when he was in the hospital. The previous night had been very restless for him. He had not slept. He had not been lucid. But he had agonized again with the intense pain that had taken up residence in his body. Now, hours later and heavily sedated, he appeared to be comatose. IV's penetrated his arms. Oxygen was being pumped into his lungs. He lay very still.

I had been sitting beside him for a long while. My hand rested on his bed. I was staring at an empty chair, lost in my own thoughts- thinking how much I loved him, how much I would miss him, and how l hurt for him. That's when I felt him move. He slowly reached out to grasp my hand. Hard. He squeezed my hand hard. I looked at him then. His eyes were closed, but tears lined his face. Tears lined my face too. And for a long while we simply held hands. There were no words. There was only silence. Yet instinctively I knew what was happening. We were both struggling to say goodbye.

EXCERPTS FROM A PERSONAL DIARY

First Day
It is the first day of July. This evening our family laughed through a delightful TV performance of YOU'RE A GOOD MAN CHARLIE BROWN. My father is coming for dinner tomorrow. He will be 65 in November. And twenty minutes ago, he called to tell me he has terminal cancer.

I didn't know how to respond. I have credentials in helping people face crises. I have studied grief. I have taught students how to minister in grief situations. I have cared for others who were struggling through the grief process. But this time I didn't know what to say. Thoughts of tragedy raced through my brain. They're still there.

My tendency is to believe the worst. I certainly couldn't disclose this to him. The doctors already have unloaded enough of the "worst" on Daddy today. He didn't need any more from me.

The first impressions of tragedy were followed by questions that surfaced almost simultaneously - Is the cancer curable? Have they discovered it in time? Will he live? How long does he have? Is he in pain? When did he first go to the doctors? How is he handling the news? Is he depressed? Hopeful? Hopeless? Then the questions became personal. Can I handle this? Can I cope with his suffering? His pain? His death? Will I inherit the cancer? Did I come across on the phone as expressing how very much I care? Did I respond to the shock the way he wanted? Was he disappointed in me? Are such questions selfish? Insensitive? Wrong? I don't know. Maybe. Probably. Nevertheless, the questions are there. And at this moment

I don't have any answers - about him or about myself. I am numb. Maybe I should take a cue from him. "I'll take it one day at a time," he said. (How many days does he have?)

We will be in limbo for another week. He is scheduled for a surgical procedure that will let us know more about the cancer. Some of the questions will be answered. The others we will work through impromptu. There is no script to follow. Now we just wait. But in the meantime, I do know that I love him. I told him that on the phone. And tomorrow we will celebrate a belated Father's Day.

Second Day
I got up at 7:00 this morning but never really awakened all day. My feelings are numb. My mind is geared in disbelief. It is true. It can't be true. Not for Daddy. Nothing like this ever happened to our family before. All day I looked forward to our "Father's Day." Hoping - hoping that seeing him, listening to him, getting more details from last night's telephone call would prove the news was

not really true. Daddy arrived at 5:15 P.M. He looked good. His mood was delightful. He had lost weight since I last saw him. Surely the news was not as bad as I had imagined. But then I learned that he has lost 16 pounds in the past few weeks without trying to do so. Would he ever look this good again? During the evening I noticed the shades of gauntness in his face. I could sense his fear in the silences of our conversation ... or was it my fear?

The added details from his doctor were not as hopeful as I wanted. I could not talk about it with him without crying. After a while the subject changed. Later in the evening I had more control. We talked again - this time around the subject.

His spirit is good. He approaches his own mortality with vigor. Even if the initial surgery confirms our worst suspicions, he wants to go for quality of life instead of longevity. I so admire him for that. It is evident that the cancer has penetrated his body but not his spirit.

Tonight I feel like crying, and at times the tears line up in my eyes. But the real cry is yet to come. My feelings for him are sure. I have confidence in him. My questions now are more for me. Can I cope with his cancer? Can I handle his death? Can I be as brave as he is? His courage is honest. He admitted he is afraid. But he is determined to make the best of it. He will. I am so very proud of him. I told him there were things I wanted and needed to talk to him about - things we've put off for forty-four years. Our talk will come when his news is confirmed, and treatment is on the way, and I have a better handle on my own feelings and thoughts.

Every member of our family hugged him when he left. He kissed each one of us and expressed his love. We did too. Will it ever be the same again?

Will he ever be back? Will Father's Day ever come again? I'm feeling pity for myself. I feel my deepest love for him.

Third Day

The tears finally came. I felt them welling up inside all morning. I could get my attention on some other subject only with extreme difficulty. But finally they came. Many of them were for the family and myself. We will have to live without him. But there were also tears for him. He so wants to live. I don't want him to suffer, to hurt. And I'm beginning to feel like a traitor for going on with "life as usual" when he is slowly dying.

Three Years Later

Daddy and I had dinner tonight at a Chinese restaurant in Oak Ridge. I noticed that he is walking with greater difficulty now. His stride is smaller, and his pace is slower. His spirit, however, remains high. We talked politics and Kentucky basketball during the meal. For whatever reason, we did not discuss heavy topics. We merely enjoyed each other's company.

At the appropriate moment, the waitress interrupted our gab with fortune cookies. As usual, I broke into mine immediately and read the words: "SOMETHING WONDERFUL IS ABOUT TO HAPPEN TO YOU" I recall thinking that was great. I always welcome anything "wonderful" that happens to me!

Daddy left his cookie alone for some time. Then, as we talked, he broke the cookie and read the message buried inside. He didn't read it out loud. He read it to himself and dropped the message on the table with the comment, "I hope so." I reached for his message and saw the words: "Time, patience, and a good attitude are healing."

Picking up on his long silence, I said, "It still bothers you a lot, doesn't it?" "Every minute," he responded. "Not an hour goes by that I don't think about cancer and death. But it's worse at night. Whenever I awaken it's very hard to go back to sleep. I lie there and think about my condition. It's like being on death row hoping for a pardon but knowing that at any moment the guards can come for you and it's over."

This sequence developed into a conversation that lasted for over an hour. We talked honestly and openly about personal matters. He mentioned how proud he was of me and how much he loved me. I responded by telling him how I loved him and how difficult it would be for me to rearrange my world without him in it. We talked straight about important matters. He expressed his anxiety about dying. He doesn't want to die! Yet he is not afraid to die. He simply doesn't want to continue the painful and diminished existence he has had for the past three years. Sometimes I cried. At other times he cried. At times we cried together. People around us were eating egg rolls and noodles and had no idea that something really special was happening so close to them.

When it was time to leave, Daddy expressed how much better he felt after our conversation. I asked him if we could do it again and he said yes. Driving home I realized that I felt better too. It was then that I knew the message in my fortune cookie had come true. Something wonderful had happened to me. For a moment, all the emotional and personal barriers between us dissolved. My dad and I were really together. We had expressed our love for each other. And not even the certainty of his death could obscure the bond we both felt in this moment.

The Spring Before His Death

Both of my sons were long-distance runners in high school, but my father had never seen either of them in a track meet. The spring before his death, Jefferson County High was scheduled in a meet at Oak Ridge and my son Alan would be running. I asked my father if he was strong enough to go to the meet. He said he was, and we made plans to attend. On the day of the meet I picked up my father. He was really too weak to go, but he insisted on going anyway. I parked as closely as I could to the track. I then helped him to a vantage point atop a small hill. He wasn't satisfied. He wanted to go down the hill to the fence around the track. I attempted to dissuade him, but my words were in vain. So, arm in arm we cautiously made our way down the hill. By the time we got to the fence, he was exhausted. The exhaustion, however, vanished when Alan and the other "milers" went to the starting line. At the gun, Alan surged ahead of the pack and led throughout the four laps. I kept glancing back and forth from my son to my father. For four and a half minutes, his pain was supplanted by pride. He straightened his body, focused his gaze upon his grandson, and cheered him around every turn on the track. After the race, A Ian came over to the fence where we were standing and talked a bit with Daddy. The whole experience energized him so that he refused to take my arm in climbing back up the hill. When I dropped him off at his house the exhaustion had returned, yet there was something exuberant about his mood. In one grandson, he had witnessed the pride he felt in all his grandchildren and, for him at least, that was worth the price of exhaustion. I also think his exuberance was related to the feeling of immortality that many older persons feel in their progeny. He knows that he doesn't have long to live, but in a peculiar sense he will continue to survive through his grandchildren.

Near The End

After months of putting my grief on hold, I've begun grieving again. The pause resulted from hope in Daddy's treatment. For months he has been in stable condition, as the medication seemed to arrest the spread of his cancer. But now it is clear that the end is beginning. A new series of radiation treatments has left him very weak. He is in constant pain. I can see the agony and weariness in his eyes. I can see it in the way he sits, and in the way he talks, and in the way we hold each other in our hello-goodbye embraces.

Daddy is now in a stage where even the medical "helps" become "hindrances." The drugs for pain hinder his ability to concentrate or remember or be alert. He is sometimes confused. He even fell last night and bruised his right hand. While the radiation is aimed at one tumor on his back, another tumor has begun growing on his neck. All of this strains his endurance and hope. This situation was compounded today as he was informed that there is some difficulty with his heart. It was simply put that way. "There is a problem with your heart." No diagnosis. No prognosis. No explanation. No word of comfort or hope. Just simply that another tumor has impacted his heart in some negative way.

On the drive home, I passed through a kaleidoscope of emotions. There was extreme grief that was deep and painful. I desperately wanted to isolate myself in a room to cry and bludgeon the walls. There was a desire to rail at God. Why? Why does death have to be this way? Why does it have to be now? I had a profound sense of shame for being preoccupied with my own pain instead of focusing upon his suffering.

A Week Before The End

For several months, Daddy has expressed a desire to visit some places that have special significance for him. I volunteered to drive him on the tour but had to wait for a time he felt like traveling. That time came today. He was still in considerable pain, yet he was determined to go. We began at his house and drove for almost three hours. We circled around Iona Circle where we lived when we first moved to Oak Ridge. I was nine years old then. I stopped the car at the spot where our house had been located and reminisced about our experiences of living there so many years ago. Then I drove to the second house we occupied in town. We followed the same process of parking, observing the location, and sharing some of our memories attached to that place. From there, we drove through some of the older sections of Oak Ridge and slowly made our way to the plant where he worked for over thirty years. I was fascinated by his stories about how things used to be.

The highlight of the trip for my father was visiting the house he and my mother built in Knox County in 1951. At that time there were only a few houses scattered about in the area. Now, there are subdivisions everywhere. He was surprised by the changes, but what interested him most was the house where we lived. We noticed each tree in the yard and remembered when we set them out as seedlings. They're now full grown. He noted that a fishpond he had built in the side yard is now gone. A bit of remodeling has slightly changed the appearance of the house. He commented about the changes, but mostly he sat in silence and reminisced in his own mind. After a long silence, his only words were, "Well, I'm ready to go."

When our trip was finished, I had to help him into the house. He tires so easily. Although he had exhausted all his energy on this short journey, he commented several times on how much it meant to him. The events of the next week confirmed my suspicions. Daddy knew he would soon die and wanted to visit his significant places before he did so. Our trip was the last time for him to leave his house.

The Final Day
When I arrived today, Daddy was struggling to breathe. He acknowledged my presence by uttering an inaudible response to my greeting. That was the last vocal message I was ever to receive from him. I sat by his bedside without leaving for seven hours. During this period he did not speak. His eyes remained closed. It appeared that he was sleeping or in a coma. The bedroom was dark. Daddy's condition and the appearance of the room had the aroma of death, and for a few hours I was very uncomfortable being there. I knew that he was dying and a part of me wanted to run away. Yet for almost six years, Daddy faced his impending death with courage. I could not abandon him now. I needed courage too.

Shortly before his death, I began massaging Daddy's arm. I didn t know if he could hear or understand me, but I spoke to him anyway. I told him once more how deeply I loved him, and I assured him that if he wanted to die he didn't have to hold on to life for me. (Sometimes persons struggle against death for the sake of loved ones and need permission to die.) From that moment he changed the way he was breathing. He no longer agonized to breathe. His breathing became slower and much more peaceful. And then it happened. While I was holding his hand and rubbing his arm, Daddy opened his eyes and looked at me. It was the first time during my seven-hour vigil that he opened his eyes. Without speaking he merely looked into my eyes for several seconds. Then he closed his eyes and took a deep, slow breath. Following what seemed to be an extraordinarily long time, he took another deep breath. This one was even slower. And then he was gone. I hugged him one last time, kissed his forehead, and bid him goodbye. I have never seen anyone die before. Daddy's death was unlike anything I have ever witnessed. This was the most peaceful and sacred experience I have ever had. In that moment beside his bed, I saw time and eternity embrace. And because of that experience I will never again fear death.

A Closing Note

Since his death decades ago, there are numerous memories of my father, both pleasant and sorrowful, that infrequently swirl into my consciousness. The memories are varied and unpredictable, but there is one that is a constant companion. It is a very comforting and reassuring memory. As Daddy's health declined in his last months, I noticed that he would hug me longer and tighter when I visited him. He ended each of my visits in the same way. He would struggle to walk to his front door and watch me until I got to my car. Then he would yell to me, "I love you." I will never forget that. His "I love you" was the last and most precious gift he ever gave me. My student, Carolyn, was right. It is hard to say goodbye!

The two experiences described above, one with a student and the other with my father, provide the existential context for the material in this book-a context that is both professional and personal. Professionally, my career involved 48 years as a university professor and mental health professional. During this time I served in two separate academic areas, Religious Studies and Graduate Mental Health. My academic training is in both areas. While teaching undergraduate courses in Religion I regularly taught a course on grief. At the graduate level, I taught future mental health professionals therapeutic techniques for addressing bereavement issues in therapy. In addition to teaching, as a mental health professional over the past four decades (licensed marriage and family therapist and a licensed professional counselor), I have done therapy with countless persons experiencing grief.

On the personal side, I have experienced grief from the deaths of several significant persons in my life. Two decades after my father's death (mentioned above), my mother suddenly died four days after her 88th birthday. On the day of her funeral, our family was gathering for lunch before going to the funeral home for her service. Our daughter Kym had not arrived, so my two sons went to her residence a few miles away to check on her. They discovered that she had been murdered. This experience became one of the defining moments in my life and in coping with the after-effects of this traumatic event I gained a totally new perspective on grief and bereavement, a perspective that now influences how I teach about grief and how I personally continue to process grief.

In the following chapters, I present my insights of bereavement within a historical and spiritual context with the hope that the material will inspire readers to craft their own understanding of grief as both gift and grace, either as one who mourns or one who cares for those who mourn.

Gone From My Sight
Henry Van Dyke

I am standing upon the seashore. A ship, at my side,
spreads her white sails to the moving breeze and starts
for the blue ocean. She is an object of beauty and strength.
I stand and watch her until, at length, she hangs like a speck
of white cloud just where the sea and sky
come to mingle with each other.
Then, someone at my side says, "There, she is gone"
Gone where?
Gone from my sight. That is all. She is just as large in mast,
hull and spar as she was when she left my side.
And, she is just as able to bear her load of
living freight to her destined port.
Her diminished size is in me - not in her.
And, just at the moment when someone says, "There, she is gone,"
there are other eyes watching her coming, and other voices
ready to take up the glad shout, "Here she comes!"
And that is dying...

Introduction

Aeschylus, an ancient Greek poet (525 - 456 BC), wrote *"He who learns must suffer. And even in our sleep, pain that cannot forget, falls drop by drop upon the heart, and in our own despair, against our will, comes wisdom to us by the awful grace of God."* The value of suffering is expressed in a similar fashion by the prophet Isaiah, *"I have refined you, but not in the way silver is refined. Rather, I have refined you in the furnace of suffering"* (Isaiah 48:10). Closer to our time, C.S. Lewis, wrote in the early 20th century, *"God whispers to us in our pleasures, speaks in our conscience, but shouts in our pains: it is His megaphone to rouse a deaf world."*

The value of suffering has been observed by persons throughout human history and one of the most common manifestations of suffering is grief. The word "grief" is a label we use for an experience that is universal and common to all persons who inhabit this planet. The label, however, is simply that-a label that points beyond itself to an array of complex human emotions and behaviors. For this reason, we must differentiate the words used to describe the experience from the experience itself. The two are not identical. Grief is not an assortment of words contained in a dictionary. It is an emotional event that is processed deep within the human psyche. This event cannot be expressed fully with words. In fact, there are some aspects of grief that are completely inarticulate, mere "groans" which cannot be uttered (Romans 8:26).

Although words cannot exhaust the complexity of the grief experience, they do enable us to understand, process, and manage the experience. The words themselves become important because they literally shape how we think about grief and influence how we experience grief. In part, this happens because thoughts shape the brain chemistry that controls our moods and behavior. Simply put, how we think about grief partially helps us to grow through grief rather than merely go through grief.

The material on the nature of grief in the following chapters is designed to address six primary learning objectives: (I) To recognize the positive aspects of grief; (2) To explore the holistic dimensions of grief; (3) To identify the nature of the grief experience; (4) To explain effective ways to process grief within a family context;(5) To describe the major aspects of caring for others who are grieving; and (6) To recognize how spirituality restores wholeness in the grief experience. In accomplishing these objectives, the information is presented in as practical and substantive manner as possible. The case studies presented in the chapters are based upon actual personal experiences. While people have given permission to use their experiences no one is identified. Names, circumstances, and other details have been altered to preserve one's identity. Sometimes the case studies are a combination of several clients' experiences.

Defining Grief

Throughout this book, grief and bereavement are used interchangeably to refer to the same experience. As such, grief is a holistic response to any significant loss. It is holistic in the sense that it affects every dimension of our being-physical, cognitive, emotional, social, and spiritual. This experience can occur with the loss of a pet, moving to a new town, the series of "lasts" in the senior year of high school or college, the loss of property or possessions, the loss of a job, the loss of health, the loss of a spouse in divorce, the termination of a friendship, the loss of mobility, the death of a loved one, or the loss of any other object for which one has developed a deep attachment. The loss can be real or imagined, temporary or permanent, avoidable or unavoidable, anticipated or unexpected. The grief response, however. always centers in a significant loss.

Grief, or bereavement, is generally thought to be rooted in the separation anxiety every infant begins experiencing shortly after birth and which continues throughout life. Contemporary research in attachment theory by some leading neuroscientists today add credence to this premise. In any event, bereavement is an ordinary element of human development which persons encounter over time.

As such, grief must be acknowledged and managed in a healthy manner. It should not be perceived as an "illness" which can be cured or prevented. Grief is the normal way we heal emotional wounds from the past as we proceed with our future.

Mourning

The terms grief and mourning are sometimes used interchangeably to describe normal responses to a loss. The words, however, actually refer to different aspects of the bereavement experience. Grief is the term that depicts the subjective feelings that attend the conscious recognition of loss. Consequently, grieving is an internal process of emotions that are felt by the individual who suffers a loss. Mourning is a term that describes social and cultural expressions of grief. The mourning process is an ongoing psychological expression of a network of emotions associated with grief, including reactions such as sorrow, anger, emotional hurt, loneliness, and guilt.

Grief Process

Erich Lindemann, in an article entitled "Symptomatology and Management of Acute Grief" was the first researcher to suggest that grief develops through various stages. He was a professor of psychiatry at Harvard, and his article was published in The American Journal of Psychiatry in 1944. He observed that grief is not experienced as a constant emotional state. It affects the mourner in different ways over time as the mourner moves from the onset of grief through the entire process. The various phases of grief collectively compose the grief process.

Grief Work

The phrase grief work was first used by Sigmund Freud and refers to the task of mourning. It is the slow and often painful experience of working through the grief process. The goal of "grief work" is to extricate oneself from distressing reactions resulting from a particular loss while establishing new and meaningful ways of living.

Basically, this is the task of finally accepting the reality of a permanent loss. According to Erich Lindemann, grief work involves three major tasks: (1) disengaging from ties that bind one to the lost love object, (2) readjusting to an environment in which the lost love object is absent, and (3) forming new relationships.

Anticipatory Grief

Grief is not always precipitated by the actual loss experience. The onset of grief occurs when the loss is anticipated. In the case of terminal illness, for instance, persons frequently begin bereavement as soon as they hear of the approaching death of a loved one. When the loss occurs, they may be in the advanced phases of the grief process. Anticipatory grief, as the phrase implies, refers to the grief one experiences whenever a significant loss is anticipated.

Complicated Grief

Complicated grief occurs when the normal grief process is denied, distorted, or delayed. Unlike normal grief, this manifestation of grief is classified as an emotional disorder and needs to be addressed by a mental health professional. This experience can be expected most often when: (1) the mourner has been excessively dependent upon the deceased; (2) there has been an ambivalent relationship (love-hate) with the deceased; or (3) there are unresolved emotional issues between the mourner and the deceased (such as unsettled conflicts). Some of the prevalent indicators of complicated grief include: (I) tendency to speak of the deceased in the present tense, (2) low self-- esteem, (3) threats of suicide, (4) antisocial behavior, (5) excessive hostility, moodiness, or guilt, (6) psychosomatic complaints, (7) veneration of objects associated with the loved one (8) resistance to any suggestion of counseling or help, (9) preoccupation with the deceased, (10) refusal to express emotions pertaining to the loss, and (11) withdrawal from others. Any of these indicators can be normal symptoms of bereavement. The diagnosis of complicated grief should be done by a mental health professional.

Going Inside

Before reading further, take a few minutes to go inside yourself. There is rich stock of memories, beliefs, experiences, insights, and wisdom stored there which you will not find in books or academic papers. Using this personal material, take some time to reflect upon your responses to the following questions:

• What are your current views (beliefs) about death, loss, and grief?

• What have been the significant losses in your own life?

• How many of these have involved the death of a loved one?

• What memories come to mind when you recall the loss?

• What emotions accompany the memories?

• Based upon past experiences, what ideas and questions do you have about grief, loss, and death?

As you journey through the information m this book, your memories, perceptions, and emotions from past losses will shape how you respond to the material presented here. Take time to explore your responses. Hopefully, they will nurture a more comprehensive and deeper understanding of your grief experiences. Remember that everyone grieves in his or her own way. The material contained in the following chapters is not intended to inform you about the correct way to grieve. It is meant to provide information that will enable you to discover grace and strength as you craft your own personal response to grief.

To spare oneself from grief at all cost can be achieved only at the price of total detachment, which excludes the ability to experience happiness.

--Erich Fromm

Chapter One

The Nature of Grief and Bereavement

Perhaps you are familiar with the celebrated parable of the blind men who perceived an elephant differently. This parable originated centuries ago in Asia and now exists in several different forms. One version has the blind man who touched the ear saying the elephant was like a fan. The one who touched the side described the elephant as a wall. The one who felt his leg said the animal was like a pillar. The one who felt the tail thought it was like a rope. The parable doesn't end there, but you get the point. All of the blind men were experiencing the same animal, but not one had a complete or adequate conception of the elephant. Their perception was shaped by their limited experience.

Like those blind men in the parable, we all interpret reality from our personal perspective and experiences. While our interpretations may be accurate, they are seldom a complete and comprehensive view of whatever we are experiencing. Humans have diverse perceptions and interpretations of anything we experience. Our perceptions may be identical, similar, or completely different. Some may be accurate or completely illusory. It is also possible that our divergent views on anything might all be true. We may be viewing an object, event, idea, or experience from a different, yet partial, angle. Our brains are not wired to adequately grasp completely the totality of all that we experience.

This common human experience applies to our understanding of grief. Over the centuries, grief has been understood, explained, and interpreted in various ways. Currently, research in several fields, such as neuroscience, medicine, sociology, psychology, and mental health, are providing new information about human functioning and some

1

of this data enables us to reframe and expand our understanding of grief and bereavement. Consequently, some traditional ideas about grief are no longer accepted. Others are enhanced or configured in a different manner. New paradigms are being formed. This is an ongoing process with grief, as it is for everything else we know about. In all areas of human experience, knowledge influences new models, theories, strategies, and understandings. In this chapter we will review some of the dominant theories on the nature of grief over the past century.

The Process of Grief

Dr. Erich Lindemann worked as the Chief of Psychiatry at Massachusetts General Hospital in Boston in the early 1940's and specialized in treating people suffering from trauma and bereavement. His research on grief was both innovative and informative. Among other innovative insights, he observed that grief was a syndrome that involved both physical and psychological symptoms, as well as establishing that grief is a process that fluctuates over time.

Since the work of Lindemann, most researchers involved with bereavement agree that there is a grief process that every mourner experiences. Yet, there is no consensus among these professionals as to the nature of that process. Some see it as a series of discrete and sequential stages. Others view grief as a process that cannot be defined or explained by distinctive and successive stages. This chapter will provide an overview of these two approaches in an attempt to summarize what we currently know (and don't know) about the nature of the grief experience.

The Sequential Model of the Grief Process

In 1969, Elisabeth Kubler-Ross, in her book *On Death and Dying*, created a five-stage model to describe the emotional reaction of terminally ill patients who were aware of their impending death. Her model, which has been applied to numerous situations since, is representative of various paradigms of grief as a process of sequential stages. Although some researchers have noted that her paradigm describes a death process rather than a grief process, her model influenced several writers to conceptualize grief as a sequence of separate stages. Some of these are presented here to illustrate the sequential stage model of explaining the nature of grief that was current last century.

Granger Westberg, *Good Grief A Constructive Approach to the Problem of Loss*

Westberg divides the grief process into ten stages. For clarity of understanding, the various stages are described separately. Yet, as is true of every paradigm of the grief process, the phases may not be as discrete in actual experience as they appear in written descriptions. In actual grief occurrences, the stages most often blend into one another without clear boundaries. The transition from one stage to another may be muted by one's emotional pain or other existential factors.

Stage One: Shock

According to Westberg, the first stage can last from a few minutes to many hours. During this period one's entire emotional system goes into shock, numbing the mourner's feelings. This automatic reaction provides the mourner with a temporary escape from the reality of the loss. The wife of a deceased spouse, for instance, may appear very serene at the funeral service. Her friends may observe her serenity and comment that she is handling the loss very well. Such observers, however, confuse serenity with shock. The surviving spouse has not yet begun to feel the emotional intensity of her loss.

Stage Two: Emotional Release

Stage two begins when the mourner realizes how dreadful the loss really is. Following the period of shock, there is an emotional release, usually signaled with the onset of profuse and frequent crying. Other emotions are felt and released as well.

You will discover an example of such a release in the diary fragments printed in the foreword. On the second day, the author wrote that "tears lined up" in his eyes. On the third day he wrote that the "tears finally came." The difference between the two experiences illustrates the transition from stage one [shock] to stage two [emotional release].

Stage Three: Depression-Isolation

During the third stage mourners begin feeling depressed and isolated. It is as though God is "not" in his heaven and things are "not" right in the world. Sometimes mourners feel that God doesn't care what is happening to them. They may even think and feel as though no one else has ever had to suffer like they are suffering. This kind of thinking allows the mourners to feel isolated and alone. For some people the feelings of depression and isolation can lift all at once. Something happens within them which triggers movement toward the next stage of grief. For others, however, this stage can drag on much longer, from weeks to months.

Stage Four: Physical Symptoms of Distress

Physical symptoms frequently accompany the grief process, especially if the grief work is obstructed in some manner. There can be such minor symptoms as headaches, backaches, stomach difficulties, or sleep disorders. More serious physical symptoms include high blood pressure, cardiovascular problems, and anxiety related disorders. There are any number of disorders resulting from unresolved grief.

Westberg illustrates the type of psychosomatic problems that can develop from grief situations by writing about the experience of "Mr. and Mrs. Brown" who lived in a small town in Iowa. This couple had a modest house and Mr. Brown worked at a job he enjoyed very much. The salary was small, but there were other benefits that provided emotional compensation for both Mr. Brown and his spouse. He came home each day for lunch, and the couple had time to putter in the garden together. He was home at five every day and they spent their evenings together. Both Mr. and Mrs. Brown lived a full and rich life, surrounded by family and friends.

In time, Mr. Brown accepted a job from a large firm in Chicago. The couple moved to this city where they lived in a beautiful apartment and enjoyed the benefits of a much larger salary. Life was good for a brief period, in spite of the fact that Mr. Brown was unable to come home for lunch every day and his wife missed him very much.

As his work progressed, Mr. Brown was required to stay downtown in the evenings to entertain customers at dinner. His wife was unhappy with this arrangement, and she became even more distressed when she learned that her husband would have to be on the road two or three days a week. The cumulative impact of all these changes began to have a harmful effect on Mrs. Brown. Prior to Chicago, her life was filled with activities with her husband, parents, brothers and sisters, friends, and small-town events. After the move to Chicago, her days were filled with loneliness and boredom. Since she was a shy person, she did not make friends nor find activities in the large city. The four walls of the apartment took on the appearance of a prison. Mrs. Brown began to resent her husband for taking the new job and secretly wished to be back in Iowa. She said nothing about this, however, because she thought she must put on a good front for her husband's success.

Mrs. Brown suffered a great loss. Yet she did not confide in anyone in person or by mail. She became engulfed in loneliness, depression, and isolation. Then she developed physical symptoms of distress: headaches, backaches, and assorted aches and pains. After weeks of suffering, she decided to go to a physician. He prescribed some medication and Mrs. Brown felt better for a few weeks, but then the symptoms reappeared. The doctor could find no physical reason for the pains and suggested Mrs. Brown enter the hospital for a complete checkup. These tests also disclosed no physical cause for her symptoms and the doctor recommended that a psychiatrist or chaplain talk to her. He suspected her difficulties might be related to a family problem. The chaplain did talk to Mrs. Brown. Finally with great emotion, she began telling him how much she hated her husband's job and the move to Chicago. Through this interview, it was discovered that her hostility, feelings of guilt, and grief were causing her illness.

Stage Five: Panicky

Mourners become panicky because they think of nothing but their loss. They might be able to think about other subjects for a moment or two, but their thoughts keep coming back to the loss situation. This hampers their ability to concentrate. Consequently, their ability to work or attend to regular activities is diminished. This in turn often makes mourners panicky that they are losing their mind or in some way "coming apart."

Stage Six: Guilt about lite Loss

During the sixth stage, mourners frequently begin thinking about things they did or did not do with respect to the loss. They also think about all the things they should have done. In the example given above, Mrs. Brown felt guilty about hating her husband's new job and the move to Chicago. Although such guilt is irrational, it is a normal part of the grief process.

Stage Seven: Anger and Resentment

During this stage, mourners get in touch with their anger. Someone or something they love has been taken away. This provokes anger toward others, the loss situation, the one who is lost, and even God. Again, much of the anger is irrational, but it is normal in the grief process.

Stage Eight: Resistance

Resistance can appear in various forms. Usually there is resistance to returning to normal routine activities. By this time, friends have all returned to their normal activities and seem to have forgotten the loss. Mourners maintain a conscious or unconscious motivation to resist this adjustment. Their resistance is an attempt to keep alive the memory of the one who is lost.

Stage Nine: Hope

At various times during the latter stages of grief a bit of hope shines through the clouds of depression. Slowly hope increasingly becomes more dominant. During this particular stage, hope is the predominant feeling. The mourner, at this point, is assured that he or she will finally adjust to the loss and go on with his or her life.

Stage Ten: Affirm Reality

In the final stage of the grief process, mourners finally begin to accept reality. They adjust to the loss and become their "own selves" again.

C.M. Parkes, *Bereavement: Studies of Grief in Adult Life*

According to Parkes the grief process has four stages. You will notice that his "stages" are much more general in nature. Rather than identifying specific emotional states of grief, he uses terms that describe the general impact of the grief experience.

Stage One: Numbness

The grief process begins with a period of emotional numbness. This stage also includes "shock." During this phase, the numbness protects the mourner from the full impact of the loss and enables the mourner to partially deny that the loss has actually happened.

Stage Two: Yearning

As the emotional numbness subsides, mourners feel an urge to recover the lost love object. They yearn to restore their situation to former times when the love object was present, and their lives were happier. I recall a dear friend who was grieving the loss of her husband to whom she had been married for almost fifty years. She would reminisce about homemaking, sharing life with her husband, and raising her children. And then with profound sadness she would lament that those days were "gone forever." During the times she reminisced about such matters, she was actually yearning for those happier times to return.

Stage Three: Disorganization and Despair

During this particular stage, mourners realize that yearning to restore the lost love object is useless and hopeless. Consequently, they give up all efforts to recover the loss. At this point, their lives become disorganized, and they have strong feelings of despair. They do not handle daily routine matters the way they used to do. This period is filled with numerous emotions and behaviors that produce disorganization and despair.

Stage Four: Reorganization of Behavior

At the onset of the grief experience, mourners lose a person or an object that is a significant part of their daily lives. With the loss, their lives become disorganized and unstable. During stage four, mourners reorganize their lives without the presence of the person or object that they lost. They resolve most of the feelings, issues, and thoughts associated with the loss. They adjust to their situation and are now prepared to go on with their lives.

J. R. Hodge, *They That Mourn*

Hodge's model of the grief process includes ten stages. With the exception of three stages, he does not present the stages in chronological order. His classification merely contains descriptions of the elements one can experience during bereavement.

Stage One: Shock and Surprise

This stage recognizes what other professionals designate as shock. This phase of grief begins with shock, or surprise, and quickly results in emotional numbness. This condition permits the mourner to slowly move into the intense feelings and difficult adjustments that are made necessary by the loss.

Stage Two: Emotional Release

During this stage mourners experience numerous strong emotions. These include such reactions as anger, hurt, pain, depression, sadness, and guilt. Mourners differ in how they handle these emotions, but all mourners experience the emotions.

Stage Three: Loneliness

In this stage, mourners become sensitized to loneliness. They experience profound feelings of being alone. They become preoccupied with the lost love object and the impact that the loss makes upon their own lives.

Stage Four: Anxiety and Physical Distress

The grief process always raises survivors' stress and anxiety levels. Sometimes the stress is accompanied by various worries, such as, what will happen to me? How will I survive without my loved one? Can I go on without the lost love object? And along with the worries, there are frequent and various physical complaints.

Stage Five: Panic

The reality that the love object is gone finally impacts mourners. Questions concerning how they will adjust or what will happen to them raise their anxiety levels to the point that they experience panic. The ensuing panic may be acute or chronic. Its intensity will vary with each mourner.

Stage Six: Guilt

It is normal for mourners to second guess and evaluate the loss experience. They ruminate about what they did or did not do for the lost loved one. Could I have done more for them? Should I have done something differently? Would the loss have happened if I had done things differently? Would it have been better for the lost loved one if I had responded differently? These and other questions frequently cause mourners to feel guilty about circumstances surrounding the loss experience.

Stage Seven: Hostility

Anger, or hostility, is a normal and common component of the grief process. Persons may be angry with God for permitting the loss. Or they may feel angry with others for their response to the loss. Medical personnel are frequent targets for such anger. It is also common for mourners to be angry with the lost loved one. This anger is irrational, but it is common. I recall one lady telling me that she was still a bit angry with her husband for leaving her. And this was eight years after his death!

Stage Eight: Suffering Silence

Mourners generally attempt to go on with their lives although their functioning is diminished by the grief experience. Persons may I live through daily routines without any or many outward expressions of grief. Internally, however, they experience profound feelings of pain and loss. As long as this goes on, their lives will not be normal.

Stage Nine: Gradual Recovery

None of the emotional states or grief stages is permanent. Mourners gradually work through all of the pain, hurt, loneliness, anger, guilt, and physical distress. The grief work of working through the various stages is the process that enables mourners to gradually recover from their loss.

Stage Ten: Readjustment

The gradual recovery ends when mourners readjust to their new situation without the lost love object. At this point, they renew normal routines, establish new relationships, and go on with their lives without the distress they encountered during the process of grieving.

Bernadine Kreis and Alice Pattie, *Up From Grief*

As the book title suggests, this model focuses upon recovery from the grief a person experiences whenever there is the loss of a love object. These two writers use three broad stages to describe the grief process.

Stage One: Shock

The grief process begins with emotional shock. This period also includes numbness. And according to Kreis and Pattie, this stage includes the onset of physical symptoms, such as sleep disturbances, loss of appetite, and crying.

Stage Two: Suffering

Stage two is a time of intense suffering. This includes the common emotions of pain, hurt, loneliness, guilt, anger, and sadness. The emotions and other dimensions of suffering begin with less intensity and increasingly progress into high intensity. The worst stage of emotional struggle comes during this third stage.

Stage Three: Recovery

From the worst phase of emotional suffering, mourners begin to experience a wane in the level of intensity. Emotional recovery results in a lessening of the hurt, pain, and sadness. Mourners increasingly become better able to handle everyday issues. They work with increased efficiency. They socialize more. They cope with grief more effectively. At the end of the recovery phase, mourners have readjusted to their loss and are able to go on with their lives.

Elisabeth Kubler-Ross, *On Death And Dying*

Resulting from her study of death and dying, Kubler-Ross observed a five-stage process that persons experience when faced with death. Some of these five stages are similar to what other mourner's experience. Kubler-Ross' stages, however, are more common for persons who receive a "terminal" diagnosis from medical personnel. The other grief processes described in this chapter describe the experience of survivors, those who lose a loved one.

Stage One: Denial

Whenever persons receive a "terminal diagnosis" from medical personnel, their first response is denial. If told, for instance, that they have some type of incurable cancer, a person may respond with the attitude, "this will not happen to me. Others may have died from th is disease, but not me. I'll beat it. I'll survive." Sometimes the victim may disbelieve the medical report and seek a second or third opinion. Denial takes various forms, yet it is the first stage in the process.

Stage Two: Anger

When a victim realizes that the diagnosis is correct and cannot be survived, denial evolves into anger. The patient may get angry at God for letting the disease happen, or at the doctor who delivered the diagnosis, or the medical staff who are unable to treat the disease, or family members, or even oneself. Usually the anger is associated with thoughts that the incurable disease is unjust or not deserved. It is common for the anger to be global and non-specific. The anger during this stage, however, can quickly become very specifically focused upon anyone who comes in contact with the patient.

Stage Three: Bargaining

The phase of anger slowly blends into a period of bargaining. The basic intention of such bargaining efforts is to hold on to life, to make one "last ditch" attempt to beat the illness and escape death. When the bargaining is with God, the patient may promise all kinds of things if the Almighty will only perform one more miracle and provide a cure. With medical personnel, it may take the form of extreme cooperation and encouragement to do or try more to provide a cure.

Stage Four: Depression

When bargaining procedures don't work and the patient finally realizes the inevitable, depression is the result. The mourner accepts the reality of the "death sentence" and becomes preoccupied with thoughts that "it is over." She now knows that there is not going to be either a miracle or some last minute cure. Nothing can be done, and death is a certainty. Depression is the immediate response to acceptance of reality.

Stage Five: Acceptance

Persons who progress through the grief process in a healthy manner finally come to acceptance. The depression ends and the patient accepts the inevitability of death and makes peace with that certainty. The person may not want to die, but he or she is no longer traumatized by death. They face it with courage and confidence.

S. Weizman and P. Kamm, *About Mourning: Support and Guidance for the Bereaved*

These authors explain the grief process in terms of five phases. Their understanding of grief is similar to that of other professionals.

However, they focus upon the unconscious behavior and major emotions of the mourner. The blending of emotions and behavior are descriptive of grief components, but they do not provide a discrete division of stages.

Phase One: Shock

These researchers agree with some others that the initial phase of grief is shock. This includes the experience of disbelief and denial. The dominant response during this phase is, 'No. This can't be true!" In addition to the denial, emotions like sadness, guilt, and anger are often present. Mourners frequently withdraw from others and become isolated. They are in touch with the horror of the situation and long for relief. The emotional experience during this phase, however, is neither intense nor lasting.

Phase Two: Undoing

Mourners instinctively engage in behaviors that unconsciously attempt to undo the loss and make things like they were before. There are daydreams that remind mourners what it used to be like. There are thoughts like, "If I had only gone to the doctor sooner," or "If I had only said no," or "If I had only responded in a different manner." During this phase, mourners are likely to engage in self-blaming behaviors or experience a sense of guilt over what they did or didn't do. All such behaviors are an attempt to undo what has happened.

Phase Three: Anger

Following attempts to undo the loss, mourners become angry. How could this happen to me? Why did this happen to me? I didn't deserve this! Mourners become frustrated. They often displace their anger, focusing it upon family, friends, medical personnel, or God. The anger coincides with a feeling of powerlessness. There is nothing they can do to change the situation.

Phase Four: Sadness

The sadness phase begins when mourners fully realize that the loss is real. This phase generally includes some hopelessness about the future: *"How can the future have any meaning without this person being there?"* There are strong feelings of self-pity and depression. And often there is a flurry of activities to distract the mourner from the pain of the loss.

Phase Five: Integration

During this final phase, mourners integrate their experience of loss into their total lives. They change their verbs from "is" to "was." They change pronouns from "we" to "I" and "ours" to "mine." The language merely reflects the emotional healing that has happened inside them. At this point, mourners adjust to the situation and go on with life.

Nancy O'Conner, *Letting Go With Love: The Grieving Process*

O'Conner describes the grief process as having four stages. You will notice that her description of the process focuses upon the major tasks that mourners must master if they work through grief in a healthy manner. You will also notice that O'Conner adds time periods to her stages.

Stage One: Breaking Old Habits

This stage lasts from the onset of grief to approximately eight weeks. During this period mourners experience numbness and confusion. Nothing seems normal or routine. There is a profound sense of unreality. And while all this is going on at the emotional level, there is a change at the behavioral level. Habits and behavior patterns established in living with someone are broken. Even casual duties, like who will make coffee or who will clean the kitchen, are disrupted. The distress at losing a loved object or person results in profuse crying and the empty feeling of being alone.

Stage Two: Beginning to Reconstruct Your Life

This stage extends from the eighth week to the end of the first year. During this period those who mourn are unable to establish normal everyday routines. They feel pain, but this diminishes over time. There are periods of depression of varying intensity. Physical tension and stress is usually high. Emotional outbursts are expected to happen. Mourners are more likely to have accidents and memory lapses. Even suicidal thoughts are not unusual.

Stage Three: Seeking New Love Objects or Friends

This stage goes from the end of the first year to the end of the second year. As the mourners readjust to their loss, they become less isolated and withdrawn. They increasingly return to normal in everyday functioning. Physical and emotional health also returns to normal. In this phase of healing, relationships with friends are strengthened and new relationships are established. Life is restructured without the presence of a lost loved one.

Stage Four: Readjustment Completed

The fourth stage marks the end to the grief process. Life is back to normal. New living conditions and necessary arrangements are made. These include all changes that enable the survivor to go on with life without the lost love object being present. The distress of the grief process and the diminished ability to cope with everyday life are now confined to the past.

Wayne Oates, *Anxiety in the Christian Experience*

Oates describes the grief process as having six stages. His model is very effective in providing an understanding of the grief experience, as well as sensitizing persons to the phases of that experience. His model provides a sense of chronicity that is lacking in some other models discussed in this chapter.

Stage One: Shock

The initial stage of grief is analogous to the shock that persons experience whenever they encounter a physical trauma. The difference is that grief triggers an emotional rather than physical shock. The purpose of this stage is to protect an individual from the full brunt of the emotional "blow."

Stage Two: Numbness

Very shortly after the initial shock of the loss, persons enter a stage of numbness. In a fashion similar to shock, the purpose of this stage is to emotionally anesthetize the person so that the loss does not create severe physical or emotional damage. At this early stage, most persons are not prepared to experience the full impact of the loss. Shock and numbness insure that individuals slowly work themselves into preparedness for processing the entire emotional trauma resulting from grief. During this stage, mourners are largely dissociated from their feelings. They make statements like, "I can't believe this is really happening," or "I feel like this is all a dream."

Stage Three: Fantasy/Reality

At this stage, persons slowly begin processing feelings associated with grief. The grieving process, however, is not constant. The reality of the loss is balanced by the fantasy that nothing has happened.

In this regard, grief is similar to the phantom pain experienced by individuals who have lost an arm or leg through amputation. It is common for such persons to feel their missing limb after surgery. The majority of amputees report sensations of itching, tingling, heaviness, warmth, and cold in the limb they no longer have. About a third experience intermittent or continuous pain. Sometimes, the sensations seem so real that the amputee forgets that his limb is no longer there and tries to stand on a missing leg or reach out with a missing arm.

In the same way, this third stage of grief is interrupted with momentary fantasies that the loss has not happened. During these periods, the mourners respond to their daily lives as usual, carrying on with routine tasks without any feelings of grief. These periods, however, are temporary. Inevitably, something will trigger the reality of the loss and the mourners will reconnect with their grief.

Oates illustrates the fantasy-reality stage with the experience of a young man who lost his wife. One afternoon, upon returning from work, the man was wrestling in the floor with his two young sons. This was an everyday ritual for the three males. They would engage in a playful scuffle while Mom prepared the evening meal. On this particular occasion, the father and his sons were wrestling as usual. The father pinned both boys to the floor and while holding them down one of his sons cried out, "Mommy, Mommy, make Daddy quit!" This plea instantly reminded all three that Mom my was no longer there. They immediately stopped the wrestling match and reconnected with their feelings of sadness.

Stage Four: Breakthrough of Emotional Pain

During this phase of grief, the fantasies dissolve and there is a flood of emotional pain. In the previous stage, feelings come and go. In this period, feelings come and stay. This is why I use the term "Pathos," a word that describes intense suffering. At this time, mourners are in touch with numerous emotions, such as sadness, anger, confusion, guilt, depression, frustration, and loneliness. It is not uncommon for the myriad feelings to be accompanied by physical symptoms, including fatigue, sleep disturbances, headaches, and other assorted minor ailments. Also, the emotional pain is so intense; mourners commonly believe they are regressing in coping with their loss.

Several years ago, I called to check on how my mother-in- law was doing. Her husband died six months previously and she was adjusting to living alone. When she answered the phone, I heard the depression in her voice. When asked how things were going, she answered that she was not doing well at all. "I think I'm going backwards," she said. "I'm not handling Raymond's death as well as I was." I knew immediately what was happening. My mother-in-law had entered the stage of Pathos. To her, the flood of emotions related to her loss gave the illusion of going backwards. This was entirely normal. In actuality, however, she was progressing through the grief process in a healthy manner. Her acute feelings of loss were painful, yet they were timely and predictable. She had merely entered a new stage in the grief process, a stage wherein all the emotions are present, and coping is much more difficult.

Stage Five: Memory / Pain

If we use the metaphor of depth to describe the

grief process, the stage of Pathos would be the deepest point of suffering. The stages preceding Pathos (Shock, Numbness, Fantasy/Reality), according to this metaphor, should be conceptualized as slowly leading a mourner into the depths of grief. In like manner, the stages subsequent to Pathos are viewed as patiently leading mourners out of the depths to the final resolution of grief.

During this stage of grief, the emotional pain of loss becomes less intense. This is reflected in the behavior of the mourner, as he or she reestablishes a normal daily routine. For brief periods of time, the mourner is able to carry on with life with little distraction from the loss. These periods, however, are dispelled by memories of a lost loved one. The memories may be triggered by a song on the radio, seeing someone at a shopping mall that resembles a loved one, an anniversary or birthday, or any other event that stimulates an awareness of the loss. With the memory, there is an immediate sense of emotional pain, and the mourner once again is thrust into the grieving process.

In this stage, however, the period of grieving becomes shorter.

Stage Six: Resolution

The final stage of the grief process is resolution. At this point, closure of the loss is established, and the mourners are emotionally able to reestablish their own lives. This assumes that the grief work of recreating one's life without the presence of the lost loved one is complete. To be sure, there will always be special memories of the loved one, as few people can completely erase the effects of the former relationship. Yet, the healing is sufficient for mourners to embrace a realignment of life, involving, if one desires, establishing new relationships, moving to a new location, creating a different style of life, or deciding to remarry. If a mourner attempts major changes Like these prior to reaching the Resolution stage, serious difficulties usually result. Only at this stage do mourners become ex-mourners. And only at this stage of Resolution are ex-mourners emotionally ready to handle important life changes.

Although every person experiences the grief process, each person proceeds through the process at his or her own pace and style. This is not to say, however, that going through the process is automatic or progressively easy. To the contrary, proceeding through the process is often arduous and slow. Patience and understanding, with yourself as well as others, is appropriate and necessary. Also, the separate stages are not as clearly discernible or discrete in actual experience as they are when described on paper. Often it is the case that the grief stages will overlap, and one has difficulty determining the correct stage. Many persons report no discernible pattern to the process at all. Sometimes grief comes in surges rather than discrete phases or stages.

The Wave Model of the Grief Process

Given the summary of the various sequential models of grief mentioned above, several observations are immediately apparent:

(1) There is wide divergence as to distinct stages in the particular models; (2) There is little agreement as to how many stages or the nature of particular stages; (3) There is no consensus as to the order of actual stages; (4) The various stages do not conform to what most persons experience in grief; (5) Every person experiencing grief does not always reach a resolution; (6) Individual experiences of grief are as varied as the sequence models themselves.

Due to factors like these, an increasing number of researchers in the area of bereavement no longer adhere to a sequential stage model of understanding grief. In 1983, for instance, Kenneth Mitchell and Herbert Anderson, in *All Our Losses, All Our Griefs: Resources for Pastoral Care,* provided a new perspective of the grief process. Among other observations, they noted that grief is not a disease or illness that needs to be cured or resolved but is an essential and normal part of life experience. In addition, they observed that the grief process does not inherently involve a sequence of particular stages. Today, many researchers in bereavement agree with this assessment. Various studies show that sequential stages of grief are not typical of what most persons undergo following a loss.

While the grief experience does involve some similarities from individual to individual, grieving is extremely personal. Everyone grieves in his or her own way and no one's experience should be forced into a particular mold that fits everyone. What most persons commonly experience in bereavement is that grief behaves more like an ocean wave that engulfs one's entire being than a sequence of distinct stages. Over time, grief, like the waves, continuously ebbs and flows. It comes and goes and there doesn't seem to be a definite or predictable pattern or schedule. Like the ocean waves, sometimes grief is calm, and sometimes it is crushing. In addition, grief appears at unpredictable times and in unexpected situations. Sometimes it washes up painful and agonizing memories and feelings. At other times it brings joyful and grateful recollections and emotions. These experiences can be interspersed with periods when life seems to go on as usual with no serious impact from the loss that's been experienced.

A Prototype of the Grief Process

Given these observations of grief from the various perspectives of both sequential stages and wave-like patterns, what can we affirm about the nature of grief itself? The following observations provide one possible prototype for understanding the nature of grief. These observations don't solve the problem of grief, because it is not a problem to be solved. Grief is a pervasive and normal human experience that needs to be understood and processed in a healthy manner. The observations provided here provide a minimal basis for perceiving bereavement in this fashion.

Grief results from any significant loss. Usually, grief is more intense with the loss of a loved one, but it is not limited to death. Grief occurs with: (1) the loss of a spouse in divorce, (2) a miscarriage, (3) moving away from home, (4) the loss of property or possessions, (5) the loss of a job, (6) the loss of health, (7) the loss of mobility, or (8) the loss of any other object for which one has developed a deep attachment.

The event that creates a loss can involve numerous qualities. Yet, whatever its nature, the grief experience always results from a significant loss, an event that "crushes" the spirit: "A joyful heart makes a cheerful/ace, but when the heart is sad, the spirit is broken" (Proverbs 15:13). This is especially the case with the death of a loved one.

Grief is a holistic experience. We are holistic (whole) beings, possessing several dimensions, including physical, emotional, cognitive, social, and spiritual. Our holistic nature implies that all of these various components of personhood are inseparably related to each other. What affects one aspect of our being affects all dimensions in some manner. Imagine, for instance, an individual who is told by a medical specialist that he or she has a terminal illness. This message affects every facet of the person's being. Obviously, the illness is a physical event. In addition, the message immediately affects the person's emotions, their relationships (social dimension), their cognitive dimension ("How will I respond to this?"), and their spiritual dimension ("Why is this happening to me?" "Will God cure me? Sustain me?"). This one medical message simultaneously affects the whole person.

To describe grief as being holistic means that it impacts one's total being. It is not merely emotional. Every dimension of our personhood is affected by the turbulent emotional undercurrents generated by painful losses. Grief is a holistic event. It manifests itself with numerous symptoms affecting every dimension of our personhood. These will be discussed in the chapter on symptoms.

Grief is an extremely personal experience. Grief is not a singular experience that maintains the same intensity, emotional reactions, and behavioral expressions from day to day or month to month.

It is a complex process which constantly changes from onset to resolution, although in many situations there may not be a complete and final resolution. For this reason, most researchers describe grief as a reaction to loss that manifests itself in diverse ways. It can be viewed as a progression of stages or as a wave-like experience that comes and goes in a somewhat random manner.

While there is no universal agreement, or clinical evidence to validate grief as having discrete stages, there is a consensus that grief is not the same for everyone. Mourners' personal experience of grief is highly individualized and seldom follows the same pattern, nor does one's experience have the same emotional intensity. Sometimes the proposed stages happen simultaneously and some of the stages don't happen at all. There is no universal pattern. What is obvious is that persons tend to grieve in their own individual manner. In this regard, the grief process is more like a wave that is full of ups and downs, highs and lows, a wave that persistently comes and recedes with varying intensity. The entire process varies over time and both the strength of emotions and duration of the process are driven by factors common to the person who is mourning.

The point here is that there are numerous variables that determine the length and intensity of grieving, including the nature of the loss, one's coping ability, the quality of the relationship with the deceased, the emotional health of the mourner, and the onset of grief. For instance, the grief process doesn't begin when the loss actually occurs. A person usually begins grieving when he or she first learns about the possibility of a loved one's death. My father was given a life expectancy of 18 months along with his cancer diagnosis and I began grieving the day he received the diagnosis. As mentioned above, this is called anticipatory grief. Because of the timeless nature of the grief experience, it is important to be patient with others and ourselves, allowing the process to develop naturally.

Healing, like grief, is a process, yet one must grieve in his or her own way and in his or her own time. The individualistic character of grief is similar to a piece of clothing. I am currently wearing a shirt that is made from a cotton blend material. The shirt has a particular color and style. There are many other shirts exactly like mine, same material, color, and style, but in different sizes. Particular pieces of clothing can be the same in every respect except for size. One size doesn't fit all. The same is true for grief. Bereavement doesn't come in one style, or one set of stages, or one anything. Grief comes in many different sizes and styles. The various elements of bereavement may be the same, but every person must experience grief in his or her own "size" because grief is tailored to fit each person individually.

Grief is a benevolent gift. Bereavement is seldom comfortable or trivial. It takes time and is painful. It impacts the quality of one's life and scars the soul. It shapes daily existence, as well as influencing physical and emotional health. It consumes one's energy and diminishes a person's ability to function in an optimal manner. One can safely conclude that grief is not a pleasurable experience. Yet, although the cause of grief is not basically a happy event, the grief process is indeed a divine gift.

One of the characteristics of our universe is that everything in human experience changes and ends. Everything from molecules to mountains are continuously in a state of flux. The ancient Greek philosopher Heraclitus (c. 535 - c. 475 BCE) expressed this inevitable and universal process in his famous saying, "No man ever steps into the same river twice." If you step into a river, step out, and immediately step back in, you are not standing in the same water you were in the first time. That water is now down-stream. Life is like that, constantly changing and moving on. This universal impermanence is also affirmed in an ancient biblical writing:

> *For everything there is a season,*
> *a time for every activity under heaven.*
> *A time to be born and a time to die.*
> *A time to plant and a time to harvest.*
> *A time to kill and a time to heal.*
> *A time to tear down and a time to build up.*
> *A time to cry and a time to laugh.*
> *A time to grieve and a time to dance*
> *(Ecclesiastes 3:1-4)*

There is indeed a certain rhythm to life. Paradoxically, one unchanging principle that governs our existence is that nothing remains the same. Life changes. All things begin, develop, and end, including human life.

How do we cope with the impermanence of life? There are several innate resources that empower us to respond in an adaptable fashion to the exigencies of daily existence. One is the fight-flight-freeze response that is inherent in human nature. In a similar fashion, God has gifted us with the capacity to grieve. One doesn't have to take medicine to grieve. One doesn't have to be taught how to grieve. We humans do it naturally. It is built into our biological system. The ability to grieve is not enjoyable, but it is natural and normal. Grief enables us to heal the past as we go forward into the future. It empowers us to cope with tremendous losses and adjust in an effective manner to a world wherein everything changes and ends. The ability to grieve is an innate gift that empowers us to endure fragile life situations. The fight-flight-freeze response enables us to survive serious threats to our existence. The grief response sustains us through significant losses as we restructure our personal world without the physical presence of the deceased loved one.

Grief contains hidden grace. The Apostle Paul once prayed for the removal of a problem he defined as a "thorn in the flesh." He did not receive the response he desired. Rather, he learned to cope in a new and adaptable manner because of God's grace: "My grace is sufficient for you, for power is perfected in weakness. Most gladly, therefore, I will rather boast about my weaknesses, so that the power of Christ may dwell in me" (2 Corinthians 12:9). The point here is that there is hidden grace in our grief experiences. The grace is not in the actual loss itself. The grace is in our response to the loss. Through God's grace we can grow through the experience, not just go through the experience. This grace-growth process will be more fully defined in a subsequent chapter.

Going Inside

As you process the material in this chapter, how do the concepts presented match your own experiences? Consider the following questions:

- Are your experiences of loss similar to any of the sequential models of grief?

- How do your experiences of loss compare to the wave model of the grief process?

- What is your reaction to the idea of grief as a gift?

- How have your experiences of loss changed you?

- How do the two models --sequential and wave-- help you to understand how other experiences bereavement?

Which of the ideas and concepts presented in this chapter have been the most helpful and insightful for you in light of your own experiences?

> *"Everyone grieves in different ways. For some, it could take longer or shorter. I do know it never disappears. An ember still smolders inside me. Most days, I don't notice it, but, out of the blue, it'll flare to life."*
>
> -Maria V. Snyder, Storm Glass

Chapter Two

The Symptoms Of Grief

There are a number of acute symptoms that accompany any grief experience. Some of these symptoms appear early or late in the grief process and take many different forms. Grief symptoms, for instance, may include the loss of appetite, shortness of breath, sleep disturbances, and headaches. It is common for mourners to suffer chronic indigestion, have difficulty in swallowing, and experience a variety of somatic aches and pains. Mood swings are common. And there might even be auditory or visual hallucinations. Clearly, the signs and symptoms of grief are as random as they are varied. Some of the more normal grief symptoms are categorized below. It should be noted, however, that many of these acute symptoms disappear after the first year of mourning. This chapter will review some of the major symptoms of grief within the context of a holistic understanding of health.

We live with the tacit opinion that we first see things the way they are and then define, or describe, them. In actual fact, this assumption is not completely true. We often define a situation according to cultural standards and then perceive it to be what we already believe, think, or assume. The way we are taught to view the world significantly influences our view of reality. Mental perceptions always shape what we see and how we interpret what we see. For this reason, scientists, as well as philosophers, theologians, social scientists, and researchers in all academic fields, create paradigms, or models, to guide us in making sense of the various manifestations of reality. There are models to explain everything from the behavior of asteroids to the conduct of zebras. In this chapter we will consider the efficacy of several models that can help us understand the various symptoms generated by grief.

The Biomedical Model

The dominant model of medical science for western civilization in recent history has been the biomedical model. This paradigm was influenced largely by Cartesian dualism, which assumed the mind and body are separate entities. Rene Descartes, a seventeenth century philosopher, crafted this prototype. According to this model, the role of psychological factors in determining health and illness are considered negligible, with much more attention being given to external agents of disease, such as bacteria and viruses, and physiological conditions. Setting aside internal psychological and emotional factors, the biomedical model largely views the body as a machine, which can be "fixed" by treating, removing, or replacing an ailing part or by destroying any external, foreign entity that is causing a problem with the use of medication. According to this medical model, grief symptoms are sometimes treated as physical symptoms (such as depression or anxiety) that can be alleviated with proper medication. While this approach may be effective in particular situations, the biomedical model does not adequately address the wide spectrum of bereavement symptoms.

The Psychosomatic Model

Psychosomatic medicine has been a recognized scientific approach for almost a century and focuses upon the interaction of psychosocial and biological factors in health and disease. This model recognizes that both mind [psyche] and body (soma] are involved in illness and distress. As such, the model broadens our understanding of health and disease since biological factors alone account for only a small number of illnesses. Cognitive and emotional factors are also involved. This model is more adaptive than the biomedical model in assessing grief symptoms, but it doesn't account for all types of these symptoms.

The Biopsychosocial Model

In recent decades, a movement in the health field has promoted a shift from a purely biomedical model to a biopsychosocial model. Research has shown that social and psychological factors influence health problems, yet these factors do not fit the narrow framework of the biomedical or psychosomatic models. The biopsychosocial model is designed to consider all pertinent factors that impact health and disease. As the name implies, "bio" includes the physical factors; "psycho" embraces the psychological (emotional) factors; and "social" comprises the social factors. While this model is highly adaptive in describing the various symptoms of grief, it still is limited in scope.

The Holistic Model

More recently, the complementary (or integrative) approach to health care has adopted an even more complete model of well-being than any of the models described above. This model views each person as a halon, a word of Greek derivation that refers to an entity that is complete or whole. With reference to personhood, halon (011.ov) refers to the physical, emotional, social, cognitive, and spiritual dimensions of human existence. All of these dimensions are interrelated and what impacts one dimension affects all dimensions in some manner. While several of the models described above use the term holistic when referring to health, this particular model more accurately represents an all-inclusive integrated approach.

As we consider the wide array of grief symptoms, you will notice that some of the symptoms are biological, others are cognitive, some are social, and others are spiritual in nature. Consequently, the holistic model is more effective in accounting for all the grief symptoms, as well as defining the nature of the grief experience itself, a response that impacts the whole person.

While we think of the various symptoms of bereavement, it is important to note that grief is not an illness and should not be treated or understood as such. It is true that bereavement can degenerate into an emotional disorder called complicated grief, but all other symptoms, such as depressive feelings, are considered normal aspects of the grief process. The fact is that grief is a normal and natural response to any significant loss and symptoms of any nature during the process do not indicate it is an illness. The symptoms merely describe the quality and intensity of the process, as well as indicating particular adjustments the mourner should address.

Categories of Holistic Symptoms

Physical Symptoms. Grief manifests itself in a number of physical symptoms, especially during the early phases of the bereavement process. These symptoms should not be viewed as unusual or uncommon. They are, in fact, predictable, expected, and normal.

Paradoxically, the symptoms disclose that one is processing through grief in a healthy manner. However, if a mourner consistently handles the emotional components of grief in an unhealthy manner, the emotions will tend to manifest themselves in physical symptoms. Also, under particular circumstances, normal symptoms can deteriorate into serious physical complaints that need medical attention. Common physical symptoms include, but are not limited to, the following:

- Headaches
- Fatigue
- Pain in the cardiovascular area
- Assorted aches and pains
- Restlessness
- Sleep disturbance
- Shortness of breathe
- Indigestion
- Loss of appetite
- Difficulty swallowing
- Declining interest in sex
- Susceptibility to illnesses such as pneumonia
- Colitis
- Worsening of chronic disorders such as arthritis
- Colds, influenza, and similar illnesses
- Migraine headaches
- Crying

Emotional Symptoms. Grief manifests a wide variety of psychological, or emotional, symptoms. Similar to the physical symptoms, these are normal and expected, mostly during the earlier periods of grief, but can appear at any phase of the bereavement period. It is considered uncommon if symptoms like the ones listed below do not occur. This list is illustrative, not exhaustive.

- Feeling down
- Depression
- Anxiety attacks
- Stress related disorders
- Anger
- Guilt
- Disorganization
- Forgetfulness
- Hopeless feelings
- Lack of motivation
- Self-recrimination
- Fear
- Loneliness
- Hostility, resentment, and bitterness
- Compulsive behaviors
- Sadness

Cognitive Symptoms. The cognitive symptoms might be included in the psychological category, but they are listed here because of their particular nature. As is true for all the other types of symptoms, the cognitive symptoms are normal and expected. They include experiences like:

- Difficulties with concentration
- Muddled thinking patterns
- Pleasant dreams

- Nightmares
- Auditory hallucinations
- Visual hallucinations
- Diminished capacity to reason effectively
- Bizarre thoughts
- Negative thoughts
- Catastrophic thoughts
- Suicidal thoughts
- Confusion
- Problems remembering things
- Inability to recall happy memories of the deceased

Social Symptoms. Persons do not live in isolation from others. Our daily routine involves contact with many other persons in numerous ways. For this reason, grief affects how we relate to, and interact with, other persons. This, in turn, triggers any number of personal interactions which can be either positive, enlivening, or negative and disruptive. The predictable types of social symptoms include:

- Tendency to withdraw from others
- Tendency to become dependent upon others
- Tendency to limit normal social activities
- Conflict with family members, medical personnel
- Increased reliance upon friends
- Impatience with others
- Increased frustration with others
- Intolerance
- Expression of anger towards others
- Diminished capacity to cooperate with others
- Diminished capacity to parent
- Diminished capacity to care for others

Spiritual Symptoms. All persons have a spiritual dimension. Our spirituality, of course, is not limited to religion. Religion is only one way that our spiritual needs and interests are expressed. The word "spiritual" refers to those qualities of existence that make us authentic human beings, as well as nurturing meaning and purpose in our daily life. As it does with all the other dimensions of human experience, grief impacts one's spiritual nature as well. Some of the normal and common spiritual symptoms include the following:

- A loss of meaning in daily existence

- A sense of disconnection

- A diminished purpose in one's life, work, and activities

- Generalized sense of injustice in the scheme of things

- Anger towards God and fear of the unknown

- A diminished interest in one's religious activities.

- An increased interest in one's religious activities

- An increased desire to discover why the loss occurred

- Feelings of personal insignificance

- A generalized belief that life has no cosmic meaning

- An enhanced effort to prove that life has a cosmic meaning

Complicated Grief Symptoms. Pathological grief occurs when the grieving process is denied, distorted, or delayed. This dimension of the bereavement process is called complicated grief because it profoundly immobilizes persons after their loss. It is also referred to as chronic or protracted grief. Persons who suffer in this manner do not proceed through the grief process in a healthy or effective manner and sometimes must be hospitalized or use medication in order to recover. It is estimated that approximately one in eleven adults will develop complicated grief after a significant loss. Some of the prevalent indicators of complicated grief are listed below.

- Tendency to speak of the deceased in the present tense
- Threats of suicide
- Antisocial behavior
- Excessive hostility, moodiness, or guilt
- Psychosomatic complaints
- Veneration of objects associated with the loved one
- Resistance to suggestions for counseling or help
- Preoccupation with the deceased
- Refusal to process emotions of grief
- Withdrawal from others
- Intrusive, upsetting memories, thoughts, and image
- Pervasive and painful yearning for the deceased

Family Symptoms. Given the fact that families function as emotional systems, grief symptoms do not manifest themselves only in individuals. The various types of symptoms affect individual behavior, and this impacts interpersonal relationships, as well as normal family interactive patterns. Whenever there is a significant loss, grief symptoms occur in the whole family system. Individual family members grieve in their own particular way. The family system also grieves in its own special way.

With the onset of grief, a family has two immediate tasks: (1) to facilitate mourning among members by providing a primary support group, and (2) to adjust to the loss my making effective changes in the way the family does business. Both of these tasks are necessary for healthy family functioning and either one can trigger reactions that ripple throughout the whole system. For instance, anxiety generated by the loss may intensify covert issues between family members. Suppose that Suzie, the youngest child, was a favorite of Mom who passed away several months ago. While Mom was alive she functioned as a buffer between Suzie and her older siblings, who were jealous of Suzie's special attachment to Mom. With Mom no longer present, the siblings decide to openly express their anger and jealousy to Suzie, resulting in considerable family conflict. The conflict, in turn, impacts the whole nuclear and extended family as members take sides in the dispute. In addition to the ripple effect of the conflict, the disharmony has an adverse effect upon the grieving process of individual family members. Family symptoms of grief include such elements as:

- A parent's diminished ability to parent
- Difficulties resulting from changing family alliances
- Difficulties adjusting to new family roles and tasks
- Unconscious attempts to replace deceased family member
- Difficulties with normal life-cycle transitions
- Intra-family disputes
- Scapegoating and blaming
- Emotional cutoffs
- Alterations of family rituals and routines
- Individual dysfunctionality resulting from family stress

There are several ways that families respond to the loss of a member. Some of the critical adjustments necessitated by the loss of a significant other include the following:

Death of a spouse. The loss of a spouse is one of the most stressful events a person can experience. Whenever this happens there are countless adjustments that must be made. The surviving spouse often has difficulty managing loneliness and aloneness. This is manifested in difficulties such as sleeping alone, observing mealtime alone, and enduring special days like anniversaries and birthdays. There also might be problems with certain times in the day. One spouse may have trouble with morning hours, while another has more difficulty with evening hours. Shortly after the loss, hallucinations, or sensing the presence of the loved one, are common and normal. Adjusting to being a single is a critical task for surviving spouses. This is especially arduous when one's closest friends are all married.

Death of a parent. The impact of losing a parent is influenced by one's age at the time of death. Younger children are usually more significantly affected than adults are. Depending upon age and developmental level, children must deal with abandonment issues, as well as feelings of guilt and uncertainty about the future. In order to help them accept the loss, children should be given the opportunity to view or touch the body of their deceased parent but should not be forced to do so. It is not uncommon for children to believe the death is their fault. In these situations, the children should be assured that they are not responsible for the parent's death. They also should be encouraged to express whatever emotions and concerns they might have. Giving children permission to feel their feelings, as well as express them, is very important. It is unhealthy for them to be praised for not crying or otherwise expressing whatever is inside them.

Death of a child. Depending upon age and circumstances, few losses are as traumatic as the death of a child. In addition to the normal grief process that is imposed upon every family member, there is added stress upon the marriage of Mom and Dad. Such a death will inevitably pull the parents closer together or drive them farther apart. If the marriage is already troubled, the loss of a child will exacerbate whatever problems exist. When the death is sudden and unexpected, as in an accident or suicide, the loss can be extremely devastating, requiring a much longer period of grief work.

There are other losses that impact on a family, losses that are largely ignored so far as grief is concerned. These include miscarriage, abortion, and prenatal death. Given the fact that these types of losses are often disregarded, there are few socially sanctioned rituals in our society for such losses and this impedes the grief process.

Death of an adult's parent. When the emotional ties between an adult and his or her parent are especially strong, the resulting grief work usually is more difficult. This is also true when the adult failed to establish normal separation and independence during adolescence and young adulthood. Sometimes, the death of an adult's parent triggers feelings of jealousy, envy, or anger among the siblings. The mirror effect is also common. The death of an elder parent might free the siblings to establish a healthier relationship with each other, especially if the parent consciously or unconsciously favored one child over another. In the case of a prolonged illness, there are frequent opportunities for adults and their parents to settle unresolved issues prior to the death. This facilitates the subsequent grief work for the surviving adult.

Variables that Influence Symptoms

Grief is one of the most universal experiences of mankind. The grieving process of persons is always similar, but it is not necessarily always the same. People grieve in their own individual ways and these ways of mourning are shaped by the culture within which people live. One person, for example, may seek out the companionship of loved ones to manage a loss. Another person might prefer to be alone in coping with a loss. The experience of grief is similar from one person to the next. The mourning process, however, is not identical from one person to another.

There are a number of variables that influence the intensity, duration, and nature of the grieving process with its accompanying symptoms. Some important variables include the following:

The length of the relationship. Ann and William had been married just less than fifty years when William became seriously ill and subsequently died. Their marriage had been unusually close, as both spouses were each other's best friend and did everything together. In fact, during the entire marriage they spent only three weeks apart. This type of relationship predisposed both Ann and William to be very dependent upon each other. During his illness, Ann spent numerous hours at his bedside caring for him. Because of this, as well as the fact that their children were grown with their own families, William's death left her exhausted and alone. In the months following her loss, Ann struggled with several illnesses. Her adjustment to the loss was compounded by the difficult task of learning how to live by herself. A major component of her grief centered upon the length of time they had together. This made it extremely difficult for Ann to reconstruct a world without William's presence.

Unlike Ann, Henry had been married for only a year when his wife Ginny was killed in a car accident. This sudden and unexpected loss thrust Henry into an extended period of confusion, disbelief, and depression. His grief was compounded by the time he and Ginny did not have together. All of their dreams and plans for a family, as well as growing old together, were obliterated by the loss. Henry's grief experience involved the necessary task of mourning the loss of his wife, as well as the dissolution of unrealized dreams.

The experiences of Ann and Henry illustrate how the length of a relationship impacts the dynamics of the grief process. The time variable always influences a loss in one way or another. This is true whether the loss involves a death, a divorce, the loss of a friendship, the termination of a job, or the loss of personal property.

The quality of the relationship. In the losses of Ann and Henry mentioned above, which one's grief would be more intense, the one married the longest amount of time, or the one married the least? One might argue this question either way. Ann was married almost fifty years. In terms of the quantity of a relationship, Ann lost more than Henry and can be expected to have more grief work to do. On the other hand, Henry lost all of his dreams for the future. His lack of time with Ginny might surely cause his grief to be more acute.

Although the length of time is a critical variable in the grief process, it does not by itself determine the depth of grief that one experiences. The quality of a relationship must also be assessed in determining how a loss affects someone. A person married for a long period of time might have endured years of abuse or neglect. This factor might create more or less grief. An individual married for only a short period of time might have experienced ecstasy and unlimited happiness. This might generate an elevated level of grief.

The nature of the loss. The circumstances surrounding a loss constitute a third variable that impacts the grief experience. Is the loss expected? Is the loss unexpected? Is the loss tragic? Is the loss natural or unnatural? Were there opportunities to resolve conflicts and other issues prior to the loss? All of these questions focus upon the nature of the loss. Usually, a loss that is sudden and unexpected is more traumatic than one that is neither, but this is not always the case. The same is true whenever there are unresolved issues with the one who is lost. All of the variables in a loss determine how one experiences grief. The nature of the loss shapes how grief will be felt and processed. This has certainly been my personal experience. My father died after a five-year battle with cancer. His death was anticipated. My daughter was murdered, a tragedy that was discovered the day of my mother's funeral. Her death was unexpected and traumatic. My mother died suddenly two weeks following her 88th birthday. Her death was unexpected, but sudden with no lingering suffering. All three of these deaths were different in a number of respects. Although I grieved deeply for the loss of each person, the bereavement process was different for each one due, in part, to the diverse variables surrounding each death.

The emotional health of the mourner. One's emotional health always predisposes how that person will experience grief. A person who is emotionally healthy usually processes grief more effectively than one who is less emotionally healthy.

Carol, a forty-year-old female, was suffering from pathological grief when a younger sister brought her to therapy. Over the previous four years, she and her sisters had lost five family members. The first was her mother. Unwilling to endure the intense pain of a serious illness any longer, her mother had committed suicide. The nature of this death severely affected the whole family, but it was especially traumatic for Carol. During the next three years, a sister died in her sleep, a brother-in-law was killed in a boating accident, and a niece was born dead. Carol did not handle these losses well, primarily because she had not worked through her mother's death. Nine months before she began therapy, her father, reluctant to live another year without his wife, committed suicide on Mother's Day. This event completely devastated Carol. She was immobilized by his death. Consequently, she quit her job and stopped doing anything for herself. She proceeded from one day to the next only with the aid of medication prescribed by her physician. Carol was unable to mourn her father's death in an appropriate manner because she was not emotionally able to do so. The number of unresolved grief experiences of the previous four years inhibited her ability to effectively adjust to this loss. Given other variables in her situation, the state of her mental health diminished her capacity to cope in an appropriate manner. If she had been emotionally healthier, she probably would have responded to her father's death differently. In any event, Carol's experience illustrates how one's emotional health impacts the grieving process.

The quality of the support group. In biblical literature, Job is the epitome of a human being who suffers and grieves. He is described as a man of "blameless and upright life" (Job 1:8). Yet, regardless of his exemplary life, Job discovered that all persons suffer, sometimes unjustly. For in a very brief period, Job lost his children, his wealth, and his health. These experiences drove him into the depths of despair. Here are a few ways that Job described his grief:

> *Like a slave who longs for the shadow,*
> *and like a hireling who looks for his wages,*
> *so I am allotted months of emptiness,*
> *and nights of misery are appointed to me.*
> *When I lie down I say, "When shall I arise?"*
> *But the night is long, and I am full*
> *of tossing till the dawn. (Job 7:2-4)*

> *I loathe my life;*
> *I will give free utterance to my complaint;*
> *I will speak in the bitterness of my soul.*
> *(Job 10:1)*

> *He has put my brethren far from me;*
> *and my acquaintances are wholly estranged from me.*
> *My kinsfolk and my close friends have failed me;*
> *the guests in my house have forgotten me;*
> *my maidservants count me as a stranger;*
> *I have become an alien in their eyes.*
> *I call to my servant, but he gives me no answer;*
> *I must beseech him with my mouth.*
> *I am repulsive to my wife,*
> *loathsome to the sons of my own mother.*
> *Even young children despise me;*
> *when I rise they talk against me.*
> *All my intimate friends abhor me,*
> *and those whom I loved to have turned against me.*
> (Job 19:13-15)

Man that is born of a woman is of few days,
and full of trouble.
He comes forth like a flower, and withers;
He flees like a shadow and continues not.
(Job 14:1-2)

My eye has grown dim from grief,
and all my members are like a shadow.
(Job 17:7)

I am hemmed in by darkness,
and thick darkness covers my face.
(Job 23:17)

In his lament mentioned above, Job expressed the misery of having to suffer alone. A strong support group would not have dissolved his grief, but such a group would have strengthened him in his grief.

Yet, that was not to be. Job's mourning was intensified because he was isolated from family, friends, and acquaintances. Even when his friends attempted to comfort him, they failed completely. At one point in discussion with his friends, Job remarked:

I have heard many words from you;
You are all miserable comforters.
(Job 16:2)

Jesus' experience shortly before he was arrested mirrors Job's experience with his friends. In Gethsemane, Jesus is described as being "sorrowful and troubled" [Matthew 26:37]. Like most persons experiencing acute grief, Jesus wanted someone to be with him. On several occasions, he begged his disciples to watch with him, but they merely slept [Matthew 26:38-41]. Jesus, as Job experienced centuries before, discovered that grief is much more intense when one does not have an adequate support group.

The experiences of Job and Jesus illustrate a common experience of humanity. The presence of a faithful and caring support group enables one to bear the pain of grief more effectively. Whenever the support group is absent or inadequate, the grief experience is more difficult.

43

The Existential Context. The existential context refers to the entire life setting of the person who has a grief experience. What is going on in this larger setting impacts how one experiences a significant loss. Robert, for example, was a twenty-seven-year-old male who was recently appointed to a significant sales position in his corporation. The new position required that he relocate to a different city. Up to this appointment, Robert lived only a few miles from his retired parents and was their chief caregiver. A week after he moved, Robert's father had a heart attack and suddenly died. His funeral was scheduled for a Saturday morning. Three hours before the funeral, his mother unexpectedly died. The father's funeral was canceled, and a double funeral was rescheduled for the following Monday. For weeks after the deaths of his parents, Robert struggled furtively with guilt for not being present when his parents needed him. Although neither of his brothers blamed him for having moved, the entire situation made Robert's grief more intense and difficult to manage. As in Robert's case, everyone's life situation impacts how grief is experienced. The existential context of one's life makes the grieving process either more difficult or less arduous.

The Age of the Mourner. Persons understand loss differently at various ages. For this reason, one's age is a variable that shapes how one grieves. We can suppose, for example, that a twenty-three-year-old female, who has been married for a year, will experience the loss of her husband a bit differently than a seventy-two-year-old female who has been married for fifty years and is highly dependent upon her husband. By itself, age is not a valid indicator of how one experiences grief, but combined with the other grief variables it does affect the grief process.

The age of children is a significant variable for the way they understand and respond to death. Judith Stillion and Hannelore Wass, in their book, *DEATH: Current Perspectives*, summarize the developmental stages for children in comprehending death. From the age of birth to three years, children usually have no concept of death. The developmental stages from approximately three years of age and above are influenced by a child's maturation, but are comparable to the following stages:

• **First Stage.** The first stage approximately ranges from three to five years. During this period, children view death as a temporary state. They are unable to grasp death's finality. Consequently, children in this age bracket may talk or think about the deceased "waking up," an event that is common to some fairy tales like Sleeping Beauty.

• **Second Stage.** This stage occurs between the ages of five and eight. Children in this age range understand that death is final, but not inevitable.

• Third Stage. The third stage begins with age nine or ten. Children at this age grasp that death is both final and inevitable.

A Final Summary

From the data presented in this chapter several factors are apparent regarding the symptoms of grief. These include, but are not limited to, the following:

• Grief involves a wide variety of symptoms that may appear. These symptoms usually impact one's total (holistic) functioning in varying degrees.

• The intensity, scope, and duration of symptoms are related to a variety of variables, such as one's age, mental health, existential situation, and behavioral responses to the loss.

• Unless an individual chooses unhealthy responses to the loss or develops complicated grief, the symptoms should be accepted as natural and healthy. Apart from complicated grief, the bereavement process is not an illness to be cured, but a normal way of healing from, and adjusting to, one's loss.

• A person who mourns can do so in a healthy manner when he or she understands the wide range of normal symptoms, accepts them, and processes them appropriately.

Going Inside

After reading this chapter, take a few moments again to process your own experiences of loss with the material presented.

• How was your experience like some of the symptoms and processes described above?

• How was your experience different? Remember that grief is a very individual experience.

• Does this material answer any lingering questions you might have about your loss?

• Does the material give you any new insights into your own bereavement?

How might these insights nurture and deepen your understanding of yourself as you process your grief?

In what ways has your losses affected your social relationships, family system, and vocational involvement? What has been helpful? What continues to be problematic and difficult? How might you address the difficult situations in a different manner?

> *The reality is that you will grieve forever. You will not 'get over' the loss of a loved one; you will learn to live with it. You will heal and you will rebuild yourself around the loss you have suffered. You will be whole again but you will never be the same. Nor should you be the same nor would you want to."*

--Elizabeth Kubler-Ross and John Kessle

Chapter Three

Caring For Those Who Grieve

John Powell, in *The Secret of Staying in Love*, wrote: "It is an absolute human certainty that no one can know his own beauty or perceive a sense of his own worth until it has been reflected back to him in the mirror of another loving, caring human being." Words like these have been around for centuries, emanating in various ways from all cultures and religions. Human beings are inherently connected and need each other. Currently, research in neuroscience is amassing significant data that confirms this observation. Our health, well-being, quality of life, and security largely depends on our relationships with one another, especially through empathy and caring.

Jesus once pronounced a blessing upon those who mourn: *"Blessed are those who mourn, for they shall be comforted"* (Matthew 5:4). Although his words appear to refer to one who experiences grief, the meaning may be just the opposite. In this particular instance, the "mourner" may be one who cares for those who are suffering, such as Jesus lamenting over residents in Jerusalem (Luke 13:34). Consider the context of Jesus' statement. He often encountered persons who were emotionally exhausted and burdened, persons who needed "rest" (Matthew 11:28-29). Regularly, he offered hope to persons barely surviving in an unjust and violent society. Life was cheap and people were trapped in a hopeless, pathetic existence, punctuated by their own apathy and indifference (Luke 13:34). His was a world where God's rule was mostly ignored. That is why he taught his disciples to pray that God's will would "be done on earth as it is in heaven" (Matthew 6:10). In this context, a "mourner" refers to one who mourns over a world wherein God's will, justice and righteousness) is in eclipse. A mourner is one who observes the sufferings of others, cares about their condition, and labors to rectify their situation according to God's will. The mourner focuses upon the aberrant plight of society in general and persons who are hurting in particular.

As a human being, do we have an obligation to care for those who are grieving, who have experienced loss? Do we have a responsibility to reach out to those who hurt? Does it matter to mourn over persons who are suffering? Of course, these questions are rhetorical, and the answers are obvious. In the first century, the Apostle Paul believed we have a divine calling to comfort those who suffer (2 Corinthians 1:3). How then do we translate this calling into practical, everyday behaviors that communicate care understanding, and support for those who are grieving? Creating a "ministry of comfort" for the bereaved does not require a degree in mental health, but it does involve several practical skills.

Nurture a genuine caring and empathic spirit.

This characteristic is not the result of genetic influence. Compassion and empathy are rooted in our human nature and are developed by loving and caring experiences from early childhood. It can, however, be developed by anyone, no matter what their early life-experiences might have been. Helen Keller, who never experienced sight, had impeccable insight into the human condition. In "We Bereaved," she eloquently expressed that our life is not in vain when we care about another's pain:

> *"We bereaved are not alone. We belong to the largest*
> *company in all the world,*
> *the company of those who have known suffering. When*
> *it seems that our sorrow is too great to be borne, let us*
> *think of the great family of the heavy hearted into which*
> *our grief has given us entrance, and inevitably, we will*
> *feel about us their arms, their sympathy, their understanding.*
> *Believe, when you are most unhappy, that there is*
> *Something for you to do in the world.*
> *So long as you can sweeten another's pain, life is not in vain."*

For a group of dispirited and dejected disciples, Jesus referred to the Holy Spirit as "the Comforter" (John 14:16, 26; 15:26; 16:7). Paul used a form of the same Greek word (1tapad:r1cm;) to describe

God's response to our suffering, as well as our responsibility to comfort others who are hurting (2 Corinthians 1:3-4). To use Henri Nouwen's phrase, we are all "wounded healers" who recognize that grief is one of life's most painful events. In order to effectively respond to others who are grieving, we must first cultivate an attitude of compassion, warmth, kindness, and empathy in ourselves. The ability to comfort others requires a genuinely caring spirit.

Encourage mourners to talk about what they are experiencing.

Some years ago, a physician made an appointment with me to talk about his wife's death, which occurred four months earlier. He and his wife had been married for twenty years and had three sons, the youngest being fourteen years old.

For most of the hour, the physician rehearsed his own grief experience, freely expressing his feelings and reminiscing about his struggle to recreate his world without his wife. "I remember how difficult it was," he said, "to make our bedroom my bedroom, and our closet my closet, and our bathroom my bathroom." With words like these, he put into words the powerful emotions of loss and the strenuous work of adjustment.

Towards the end of our session, the doctor mentioned a particular concern about one of his children. "Since my wife died, both of the older boys have cried and talked out their feelings. The youngest boy, however, has yet to cry and he refuses to discuss his mother's death. I need some help in knowing how to respond to him."

The father had mentioned earlier that he was planning to attend a medical convention in California two week hence. I asked if he could take his younger son on the trip, and he said that wouldn't be a problem. My suggestion was that during the trip he carve out some time alone with his younger son. At some appropriate moment, I encouraged him to ask his son if he missed his mother. If the son responded, he was to encourage him to talk about it. If the son refused to respond, I asked the doctor to respond with something like, "Well, I sure do," and then tell his son what he had told me about his struggle to make "our bedroom my bedroom."

The strategy that I recommended to the physician was based upon two accepted principles: (1) At some point in the grief process, health is generated by expressing one's emotions; and (2) When we disclose something very personal to another person, the other person is more likely to respond by divulging something personal about himself or herself. In this particular situation, the father had not disclosed his own struggle to his sons. By doing so, I thought his disclosure might trigger the same from his younger son, a strategy that worked in this situation.

This physician's experience with his young son illustrates the value of expressing one's grief in an appropriate way and at the appropriate time. I refer to the *appropriate* time because persons are different, and some are more accustomed to verbalizing feelings than others. Males especially are prone to mask their feelings and this tendency sometimes inhibits their grieving. In any event, persons should be encouraged to talk about their experience of loss, but not *pressured* to talk about it.

Whenever persons express their grief in an emotionally safe environment, several positive results can nurture the health benefits of the bereavement experience. Each time persons recount their story they gain new insight into what they are experiencing. This facilitates emotional healing. In addition, current research in the area of neuroscience suggests that grappling with issues such as this can enhance healthy brain functioning, as well as facilitating spiritual growth. Both of these enable persons to grieve in a healthy manner.

Be attentive to, and accepting of, what mourners say

In order to help mourners grieve, we encourage them to talk out their feelings and accept what they say, no matter how painful or unrealistic it might be. This runs counter to a common practice in our culture, for people often are inclined to invalidate or minimize the feelings and beliefs of others in order to "cheer them up" or "make them feel better." This practice, however, usually has the opposite effect. Whenever we invalidate another's feelings or beliefs, they tend to become defensive or to stop talking altogether. When we accept what persons say, whether we agree or not, we encourage them to continue talking. Keep in mind that accepting a statement doesn't mean agreement with the statement.

Consider this interaction between a hospital patient and a concerned friend. The patient has been ill for months, suffering from a congestive heart disorder. His prognosis is not good, and he is depressed, as well as being hopeless about the future. "I don't have anything to live for," he sighs, "there's no reason to go on." His friend is dismayed by this comment and responds, "That's not so. You have a lot to live for. Think about your job. And what about your kids? They need you." This response is intended to make the patient feel better and to brighten his prospects of the future. In fact, it is likely not to change his opinion nor make him feel better. The remark, however, will likely reduce the patient's willingness to express how he really feels and thinks.

Notice the same interaction wherein the friend responds appropriately, accepting what the patient has to say. The patient laments, *"I don't have anything to live for. There is no reason for me to get well."* The friend responds to the hopelessness behind his words:

"That's a miserable way to feel isn't it?.,

"You bet it is" says the patient. "I lay awake at night agonizing over this."

"I'm sure. Not having a reason to go on is a tough way to live, ..

"I've never felt this way before. I just want to crawl off somewhere and die."

You will notice in this interaction the friend does not minimize or invalidate the patient's expressions. By accepting what the patient says, the friend facilitates the patient's ability to continue disclosing his deepest thoughts and emotional pain. The key here is empathic listening. The goal of the friend is not to make the patient feel better or think more logically. His purpose is to enable the patient to ventilate his feelings in an emotionally safe environment, a process that is healing in itself. This is an effective way to help mourners. Encourage them to talk and then accept what they say.

51

The objective of supportive listening is to hear, understand, empathize, and support the mourner. Whenever we invalidate, minimize, or discount another's feelings, beliefs, or experiences we cease to be comforters. Remember Job's reaction to his alleged friends. As he struggled to make it through each day his friends offered empty words rather than a supportive presence. Frustrated, hurting, and feeling abandoned, Job lamented: "*I have heard many things like these; miserable comforters are you all!*" (Job 16:2). Job's friends offered platitudes, but not themselves. A helpful comforter displays a supportive and attentive attitude.

Avoid Pat Answers and Elicits

Another common response to mourners is to offer pat answers for complex situations, answers that ultimately do nothing to ease emotional pain. Some of the common cliches given to those who suffer include:

"It could be worse."

"A lot of people have to suffer."

"Think about those who have it worse."

"It's God's will."

"Just trust in the Lord."

"Think about something positive."

"Just get your mind off it."

"All things work for good."

"It's not so bad."

"You've got to be strong."

"Don't cry."

"Think positive."

"Don't think about yourself."

Mourners often report that cliches like those above do not help and in many cases trigger negative reactions. The reason such responses do not help is because mourners are not looking for pat answers. They are looking for and need emotional support from those who care. Cliches do not satisfy this need. If a comforter doesn't know what to say, he or she can say something affirming like this: *"I don't know what to say, but I do want you to know that I care."*

Pat answers and cliches are unable to meet the needs of mourners because they do not lessen the acute emotional pain of grief. Persons usually employ cliches because they either do not know what to say or do not care to address the critical issues of the grieving process. To use the words of Job, although their intentions are commendable, those who use cliches are "miserable comforters."

Be Available

Perhaps simply being present for the mourner is one of the most effective ways to be a comforter. Being present means being available in a caring, supportive, and understanding manner. Remember Jesus' experience? In Gethsemane the night of his arrest, Jesus was "sorrowful and deeply troubled" (Matthew 26:37). Like most persons experiencing acute grief, he wanted someone to be with him. On several occasions that night, he begged his disciples to watch with him, but they merely slept (Matthew 26:38-44). Coping with deep emotions is always affected by the quality of one's support group. The presence of a faithful and caring support group, even if the group is only one person, enables the mourner to bear the pain of grief more effectively. Whenever the support group is absent or inadequate, the experience for the mourner is more difficult. Effective comforters provide an affirming presence.

Whenever a death occurs, there is usually an immediate outpouring of care from friends and loved ones. This care takes the form of visits, cards, flowers, food, emails, and the like. Such care continues for several weeks, as friends check out how the mourner is coping. Yet, by the time mourners enter the mid-stages of the grief process, times when they need a support group the most, their friends usually are not as sensitive to their loss. This is why it is important for effective caretakers to be available throughout the whole bereavement process.

Being available means that one is sensitive to, and anticipates the needs of, the mourner. This ability is manifested in practical ways, such as making regular phone calls or visits to see how the mourner is coping, inviting the mourner to lunch, or asking if they need any help. Being available is as simple as asking, *"How are you doing?"* or *"Would you like to take a drive to the mountains?"* It also is expressed by assuring the mourner, "Any time you need me, please call." And, of course, being available means responding whenever the mourner does call. On special days, such as birthdays, holidays, or anniversaries, being available is expressed by assuring the mourner, *"I thought this day might be difficult for you and I just wanted you to know that I am here for you."*

Provide Opportunities to Re-grieve

Re-grieving is the process of reminiscing about the loss. This is a painful experience for mourners, but it is healing because it enables them to process all the emotions resulting from their loss. Re-grieving also enables mourners to adjust to the loss.

Opportunities for mourners to re-grieve may be created by certain pivotal questions, such as *"What is your most difficult struggle at this point? What do you miss the most? Can you identify all of the emotions you are feeling now? Tell me again about the day he died? What happened? How did you react? What did you think? How are things different now? What are your happiest memories of him? What are your most painful memories of her? If you could do it all again, what would you do differently? If you could speak to her once more, what would you say? What have you learned about yourself through this loss? Which of your emotions are most difficult to handle? What are your most troublesome moments? How is the loss changing you? What are the biggest changes this loss will mean for your future? What do you fear the most?"* Of course, one shouldn't ask all these questions at one time or overburden the mourner with any questions when he or she is not open to reminiscing or talking. These questions are merely the types of questions which, when appropriate, can be used to help the mourner re-grieve.

Offer Practical Help

Providing practical help is appropriate at any time during the grieving process, yet it is especially beneficial during the earlier phases of grief. There are numerous tasks that have to be managed whenever a death occurs. Unfortunately, some tasks have to be completed when the mourner is not living in an emotionally optimal manner. Practical support can be extremely helpful during this time. Baby-sitting, house sitting, making phone calls, preparing food, and running errands for mourners are only a few activities that free them to take care of more pressing matters.

Display Patience

Some years ago, I was working with a client who had lost her husband in a hunting accident. After struggling with her grief for a year, the woman appeared for her counseling session in a highly agitated state. During the previous week, two of her closest friends told her that she had been "wallowing" in sorrow long enough. The friends declared that grieving for a year was sufficient. Now it was time to go on with her life. These words greatly distressed my client because she was unable to continue life as usual, and she believed something was wrong with herself because of this. I assured my client that her friends were speaking out of their own frustration. There was nothing wrong with my client. There was something inadequate about her friends' view that a "year was long enough to wallow in sorrow." They were ignorant of the grieving process and consequently had lost patience with the mourner.

Mourners need patience from their supporters in several areas. Sometimes they project their emotions upon those closest to them. Anger, for instance, may be misdirected towards a supporter rather than to the one who is the object of the anger. Sometimes a supporter may be convinced that the mourner is not processing his or her grief in an appropriate manner or that the mourner is becoming too dependent. There are various ways supporters can become aggravated and frustrated with mourners. It is important to remember that mourners must process grief in their own ways and according to their own emotional schedule. As in the case reported above, for instance, a year is not sufficient time to proceed through the grief process. It is important to know that mourners are not responsible for pleasing their supporters. Supporters are primarily responsible for helping the mourners. For this reason, supporters need to display a proper amount of patience when caring for those who have suffered a significant loss.

Going Inside

After reading this chapter, consider your own responses to those who are grieving.

• How do you typically respond to those who are experiencing grief?

• How do your responses correspond to the suggestions offered in this chapter?

• What behaviors have you found helpful in caring for others?

• What possibilities does this chapter raise for you in terms of caring for others?

> "If you are looking for special words to comfort
> someone grieving, look no further than within
> your heart. Forget the cliches or any packaged
> sayings; it's important to be genuine. Your goal
> should be to express compassion, not to cheer up
> someone who is recently bereaved."
>
> -Mary Beth Adomaitis

Chapter Four

Personal Grief Management

As mentioned above, Henri Nouwen referred to Christians as wounded healers. Both words are significant for those of us who care about grief. We are "healers" in the sense that we minister to others in a caring and compassionate manner that facilitates their healing. We are also "wounded" because we are not immune to the inevitable sufferings of this world. So far as grief is concerned, we must all experience the depths of emotional distress and agonizing pain that accompanies loss. This means that we must learn how to adequately manage our own grief.

T. B. Maston, in his book *How to Face Grief,* observed that grief is the "flip side" of love. if there were no love, there would be no grief. It frequently happens that the intensity of grief is directly related to the depth of love one has for the lost love object. One dimension of bereavement, in this regard, is self-grief. We are sad for ourselves because we have lost someone or something that we care deeply about and need. We are anxious because our world has changed drastically, and we have to make life-changing adjustments. How then do we cope with our own wounds and challenges? The reality that humans can become stronger through all types of suffering has been recognized for centuries. Grief is certainly one form of adversity. How do we grow through the bereavement process? There are countless ways we can develop in healthy ways through this experience. This chapter will focus upon several healing responses to a significant personal loss.

Be Open about Death

For a large segment of our population, death continues to be a very difficult topic to discuss. Unfortunately, this is true for professionals as well as laypersons. The reality of death makes us uncomfortable.

Consequently, we are hesitant to think or talk about death, especially with someone who is dying. Our response to death, in this regard, is called denial.

Our denial of death is expressed in several ways. One common practice is to ignore the issue when talking with one who is dying. My father and I discussed this topic several times before his death. He was exasperated with friends who visited and totally disregarded his condition. Their refusal to talk about his disease created intense feelings of uneasiness and left him frustrated. To be sure, persons who ignore such discussions probably do so to protect the patient, as well as themselves, from unnecessary distress, but this intention is misguided. Those who are dying need and usually desire to talk about their condition. Processing one's thoughts and emotions regarding a terminal illness is one-way patients adjust to their situation.

Denial of death is also expressed through our euphemisms for this experience. Rather than using the word death, we speak of *sleeping, passing away, going on, going to a better place, going to Heaven,* or simply *passing on.* All such euphemisms are intended to remove the finality and irreversibility from death. These euphemisms obscure the reality that death is as normal as birth. Contrary to popular opinion, life and death are not opposites. Both birth and death are two extremes of life. Death is difficult, but it is just as normal as birth.

Mourners effectively manage their own grief when they forgo denial and become open about death. The most efficient way for us to do this is to accept our own mortality. In training caregivers how to respond to mourners, I initiate this process by having caregivers write their own obituary. This exercise inevitably triggers one's fears, uncertainties, and anxieties about death. By openly talking about these reactions in the group, caregivers begin to cognitively accept their own mortality, an accomplishment that facilitates their ability to care for mourners.

Like caregivers, mourners process their grief by identifying, accepting, and expressing their anxieties about death. Accepting our own mortality and diminishing our fears about death enables us to heal the emotional pain caused by significant losses. We can more effectively manage grief by thinking and talking about death in realistic terms.

Participate In Death Rituals

Human beings, both ancient and contemporary, mark significant events with certain rituals. This is particularly true of death. We have numerous rituals to mark this pivotal experience. These death rituals provide a context for understanding the loss and furnish guidelines for the social expression of our grief.

Forty years ago, my grandfather died. He was one of the most significant persons in my life, having provided an immense amount of emotional security throughout my childhood, and his death had a profound effect upon my life. Because of my position in the family, I was asked to arrange his funeral. I readily accepted this responsibility and planned every detail of the service to the best of my ability. In one respect, however, I failed. I didn't fail my grandfather. I failed myself for I decided not to view his body. I wanted my last memories to be of him being alive and not dead. I didn't recognize the subtle presence of denial. At the time, I reasoned that this was appropriate and normal. For some persons in particular situations it might be normal, but I was not that person nor was this an acceptable situation. Again, the grief process is a very individualized experience.

In the weeks following my grandfather's death, I began to experience an unexpected reaction. I went about daily routines without being unusually afflicted with acute sadness. I knew that my grandfather was dead, but this intellectual realization did not penetrate to my emotions. One morning, however, my mood changed. I developed an intense yearning to visit his grave. That day I skipped lunch and followed this powerful inclination. For almost an hour, I stood at his grave, crying and telling him how I missed him and loved him. I thanked him for all he meant to me, as well as all he had done for me. My conversation at his graveside contained all the things I would like to have told him before he died. That conversation provided the incentive for me to progress through bereavement in a healthier manner.

Looking back on this experience now, I recognize the psychological significance of the visit to my grandfather's grave. By refusing to view his body the night before his funeral, I impeded my acceptance of his death and strengthened the denial that the event occurred. Visiting his grave dissolved the denial and emotionally verified the reality of his death, as well as providing the repressed permission for me to grieve.

My difficulty grieving my grandfather's death resulted from not observing the necessary death rituals. Although it may not be true for everyone, not viewing his body at the appropriate time diminished my ability to fully accept his death. I knew intellectually that he was dead, but I did not embrace that fact emotionally. If I had participated in the viewing ritual, I think I would have experienced his death at an emotional level and would not have needed the therapeutic visit to his grave. This is because the rituals of death provide a framework wherein we can express grief in a healthy and effective manner.

As long as forty thousand years ago, pre-historic people placed their dead in a fetal position, covered the body with red ocher, and buried the body in shallow graves along with personal relics. Years ago, in a jungle on the island of Mindanao in the Philippines, I witnessed a ritual of the Manobo people as they enclosed a deceased tribesman in a carved-out tree trunk. Prior to burial, they sat all night with the corpse, beating drums to frighten away evil spirits. In the Middle East, family and acquaintances sometimes walk in a procession behind the casket and loudly moan and wail, publicly expressing their grief. In Eastern Kentucky, mourners often conclude a funeral by walking past the casket to view the body one last time and then leave the building, permitting the family to have their last view in private. In central Mississippi, mourners do the same, but go back to their seats rather than leaving the building. The community thus symbolizes the support they have for family members as they take a final view of the deceased. People of all eras and in all places have developed death rituals. The rituals differ from place to place and from culture to culture, but the fact remains that all humans have certain rituals that provide a framework for mourning the death of a person.

Some of the common death rituals in American society include:

(1) a gathering of family members, (2) the community responding with caring behaviors, such as preparing and bringing food to the family, (3) the family receiving friends prior to the funeral, (4) sending cards and flowers to the family, (5) viewing the body of the deceased, (6) a public funeral to mark the death experience, a service which also includes numerous rituals, (7) a procession to the burial site, and (8) a public or private burial or cremation. Rituals such as these have slight variations from place to place, as in the case of viewing the body of the deceased in Kentucky and Mississippi. Whatever rituals are involved and whatever form they take, all rituals provide a suitable framework for survivors to mark this significant transition in human life. Participating in death rituals facilitates a mourner's ability to grieve in a healthy and effective manner. Mourners should not be forced to participate in funeral rituals, but for most persons the rituals are beneficial.

Establish Closure with the Deceased

One of the tasks of grief work is to disengage from the emotional ties that bind oneself to the deceased. Given the variables in a particular situation, this may or may not be possible to do completely. Bereavement is not an illness to "get over." Sometimes an ultimate and complete resolution is not possible. Nevertheless, personal disengagement must be invasive enough to enable survivors to redefine their world without the presence of the deceased. Until this task of grief work is accomplished, a person cannot respond to the grief process in a healthy manner. And to clarify this further, disengagement does not mean the end of the relationship. We retain a relationship with the deceased even though they are absent. Disengagement means recalibrating our everyday world without their presence.

At fifty-four years of age, Edna was in her second marriage. Her first husband was suddenly killed in an accident at work. Before completing her grief work, Edna met and married Rev. Smith, a minister who had lost his wife to a long struggle with cancer. Edna and Rev. Smith had been married for seven years. Even after this period, Edna continued to address her husband as "Reverend

Smith." Surprisingly, she also addressed her husband as "Reverend" during intimate moments at home. In their bedroom, Edna kept a large photograph of her first husband on top of the dresser, as well as his pocket watch, wound and with the correct time. Behaviors such as these inhibited any growth in her relationship with Rev. Smith. Edna was unable to embrace her new marriage because she had not established closure with her first husband.

Although Alice's experience was different from Edna's, she also lived a diminished existence due to failure to establish closure with the deceased. In her case, the deceased was a son who was killed in an accident. In the three years following the son's death, Alice consistently refused to go through his possessions. They were all stored in his room, which was scrupulously kept just as he left it. Family members, who survived the boy's untimely death, were not permitted to speak of him at any family function. To do so would admit the reality of his death, a fact Alice refused to accept. As a result from her failure to grieve in an appropriate manner, Alice developed physical, emotional, and spiritual problems. She was chronically ill with assorted physical disorders, experienced clinical depression, and became obsessed with the loss of her own salvation. All of these were triggered by her inability to establish closure with her deceased son.

When a person progresses through the grief process and completes his or her grief work, closure with the deceased is normally established. There are, however, occasions when closure is inhibited, usually due to unresolved issues with the deceased. In such cases, the issues must be resolved before closure can be attained. Also, as indicated above, closure does not mean the end of a relationship. At various times, and in differing intensities, persons may experience waves of grief as long as they live.

Whenever past issues need to be addressed and healed, several techniques are available. One might make several trips to the grave and talk to the deceased. One might "speak" to the deceased through visualization or supposing that the deceased is sitting in an empty chair. Writing out one's feelings in a journal is often helpful. In some circumstances, formally marking the loss might be effective. Writing letters to the deceased, mentioning painful memories and expressing one's feelings, also facilitates the healing of unresolved issues.

Betty and Ralph resolved issues surrounding a miscarriage, which Betty had twenty-five years earlier by formally recognizing the unborn son's death. Although this young couple was to have four other children, this was their first pregnancy, and both were elated at the prospect of becoming parents. Six months into the pregnancy, Betty began having difficulties that resulted in a miscarriage. The experience was acutely painful for both, but especially so for Betty. Every year thereafter, she developed a severe depression each year on the anniversary of the miscarriage. This had been going on for twenty-five years when she told me about her reaction. After discussing possibilities of resolving this situation, Betty and Ralph decided to address their unresolved grief by formally making the deceased son part of their family. In a special ceremony, which the parents asked me to witness, Betty and Ralph completed the following certificate, both naming and claiming their unborn son. The "naming" ritual enabled Ralph and Betty to create a different way of perceiving their family, thinking in terms of having five children rather than four, with one child having died and four still living. Through this simple ceremony, closure with the unborn son, "David," was established.

Among other results of closure, Betty's annual depression over the miscarriage never returned.

Establishing closure with the deceased does not mean that loved ones are forgotten or that they are unloved. Death doesn't end a relationship with the deceased. In some fashion that relationship will remain part of us as long as we live. Closure, however, does mean that the emotional pain of the loss is accepted, and we adjust to the physical absence of the loved one in our everyday world. In time, establishing closure enables survivors to resume their lives without being crippled by the loss.

Process Your Emotions

Our society often underrates the value and importance of emotions. This is expressed by decrees admonishing us to ignore, deny, distort, rationalize, intellectualize, or invalidate our feelings: "*You shouldn't be* angry." "Don't cry." "Smile and act like nothing's wrong." "Be strong." "Get your mind on something positive." "Think about something else." "Get busy and do something." "Don't think about yourself." The unspoken message in statements like these is simple and direct: "It's not OK to feel your feelings." This message is not intended for one gender. It is crafted for both males and females. Males frequently are told outright that feeling emotions is weak and un-masculine. Males are not supposed to hurt, cry, lose control, or admit frailty. They are to be rational, not emotional. They are to appear strong rather than weak.

Females, on the other hand, are permitted to express emotions in our culture, but this freedom is generally perceived as a sign of weakness. Because they display emotions more readily than males, females are labeled "emotional" or "hysterical," both terms denoting something inferior to "rational" and "logical."

Although emotions often are depreciated in our society, they, in fact, serve a vital function in maintaining emotional and mental health. Emotions energize us to cope with the changes in everyday living. Research data confirms that individuals who process their emotions appropriately are healthier and live longer than other persons. This fact is particularly true for those experiencing grief. Processing the feelings associated with grief facilitates grief work and enhances the mourner's physical and emotional health.

Several years ago, I was the keynote speaker for a church conference in Washington, D.C. Following one of my presentations, a woman in her late forties cornered me in a hallway and began to unburden her difficulties resulting from her father's death several months prior. It was apparent that she had processed none of the feelings related to his death. One particular irritant was her anger at God for permitting her father to die. This aspect of her experience was inhibiting a normal grief process. I asked the woman to consider telling God about her anger. With my reassurances that he would understand and not wreak vengeance upon her for doing so, she did what I asked. Three days later, she confronted me again in the hallway. This time, however, there was a marked difference in her mood and attitude. By "owning" and expressing her anger toward God, the obstruction to a normal grief process was removed and she was able to feel her grief.

Processing emotions related to grief is accomplished simply by feeling your feelings, no matter how painful they might be. This means crying when you feel like crying, and being inactive when you feel exhausted, and being weak when you feel drained, and being angry whenever you're angry. It means identifying, owning, and appropriately expressing whatever you feel. And it certainly means talking out your feelings, fears, uncertainties, frustrations, and confusion whenever any of these are swirling in your mind. Masking or denying your emotions impedes the whole grief process, often contributing to emotional or physical problems. Processing your feelings, however, facilitates the entire grief process, enabling you to be emotionally and physically healthier. Processing emotions in appropriate ways is not always easy or simple, but it is a healthy way to manage grief.

Affirm and Care for Yourself

Self-recrimination and self-doubt are often an integral part of the grief process. There are times when survivors question whether they could have, or should have, responded to the deceased differently, particularly if the deceased suffered with an illness prior to his or her death. It is common and normal for survivors to judge themselves negatively for how they responded to the deceased in the days or months preceding the loss. In the days following my grandfather's death, for example, I berated myself for not having visited him before his death. I had scheduled a business trip to a city four hours away on a particular Friday and planned to visit him on the way. However, I got away from the office late and decided to postpone my trip to see him until the following Monday. I never got to see him because he died early Sunday morning. That postponed visit was transformed into guilt, as I kept thinking, "I should have visited him on Friday." Sometimes a significant loss triggers memories of behavioral patterns that were perpetuated over a long period of time, patterns that were less than desirable. A mourner may feel guilty over never having established a close relationship with the deceased, or for maintaining a distant relationship.

Mourners also often feel guilty, or demean themselves, for some of their feelings that are generated by the loss, emotions like anger, hostility, jealousy, or bitterness. Such emotions are normal and are as appropriate for the deceased as they are for the living.

Whatever creates negative feelings or self-recrimination, mourners need to give themselves permission to feel their feelings and accept their failures. This involves affirming themselves. Guilt and self-recrimination are routine and do not mean that the mourner is a bad person. There are many things we would do differently if we had reliable knowledge of the future. The fact is, however, that we do not have such information. This means that numerous memories are likely to surface, which generate guilt, memories wherein we regret doing this or that. In the grief process, we must admit all of the "could's and should's" and resolve them. We do this by affirming ourselves and forgiving our past.

Renew and Deepen Relationships

During the early phases of bereavement, there is a natural tendency to withdraw from social relationships with others. Life is disrupted and nothing goes on as usual. In these early phases of grief, mourners are galvanized to their loss and build their lives around the loss. This focus upon the loss enables them to process their grief appropriately. As bereavement progresses, there is a need to restore one's social and work routines. This involves forming new relationships and deepening old ones. In the beginning of this process, survivors often feel they are being disloyal to the deceased. At times, they hesitate to

cultivate social relationships for fear the deceased will be forgotten. Both of these fears are understandable, yet unfounded. Developing new relationships is not disloyalty to the deceased and there is little evidence that survivors forget their loved ones. No one will ever replace a significant other in your life. Although grief work involves severing emotional ties to the deceased, that person will always maintain a special place in your mind. In reality, the formation of new relationships enlarges your inner world to accommodate the presence of new significant others. These persons enrich your life, as the deceased did, and compensate for the absence of the loved one.

Maintain and Nurture Spirituality

Individuals understand and express spirituality in diverse ways, yet it is an obvious fact that human beings are inherently spiritual beings.

Because it incorporates a sense of meaning and purpose, spirituality is especially animated in times of emotional stress, physical sickness, mental illness, loss, and death. These experiences typically threaten, weaken, and destabilize our sense of well-being, resulting in a diminished quality of life. Given this tendency, maintaining and nurturing our own spirituality can be very helpful in coping with adverse life situations. This is particularly true for bereavement.

In the more intense phases of bereavement, some mourners commonly experience the absence of God, if not apathy from God for permitting the loss. I recall the response of a mother to the critical illness of her young son. The boy was suffering from an rare physical condition and the mother prayed continuously for his recovery, with all of the prayers unanswered. Aggravated by this experience, she remarked that Jesus healed many persons during his life and wondered why he couldn't, or wouldn't, perform one more healing for her son. At one point in her lament, she asked, "What does God do, anyway?"

This mother's struggle with God's apparent apathy was not a rejection of faith. Her obvious dissatisfaction with God was just the opposite. It was a manifestation of faith, a disclosure of faith that is misunderstood by some, but consistent with ancient Hebrew piety. Over a long period of time, these people collected a large number of songs which are now contained in the book of Psalms. Scattered among these hymns is a group of songs which are designated as "laments." These hymns provided a device for the Hebrews to rail at God for the seeming injustice of their suffering. These primeval people recognized that struggling with God over their personal distress was in itself an act of faith and piety. The existence of the lament songs also presupposes that God, in his mercy, understands and permits his people to be upset with life's painful experiences. He does not take offense at our impious thoughts and words, nor is he threatened by the anger we might project upon him because of our grief and anguish.

The lament psalms characteristically began with an address to God for his inaction, followed by a complaint for corporate or personal suffering. After the protest, however, the hymns end with an affirmation of faith. The following is one example of a lament psalm.

Notice the pattern which proceeds from complaint to affirmation.

> *How long, O LORD? Wilt thou forget me forever?*
> *How long wilt thou hide thy face from me?*
> *How long must I bear pain in my soul,*
> *and have sorrow in my heart all day?*
> *How long shall my enemy be exalted over me?*
> *Consider and answer me, O LORD my God;*
> *lighten my eyes, lest I sleep the sleep of death;*
> *lest my enemy say, "I have prevailed over him";*
> *lest my foes rejoice because I am shaken.*
> *But I have trusted in thy steadfast love;*
> *my heart shall rejoice in thy salvation.*
> *I will sing to the LORD,*
> *because he has dealt bountifully with me.*
> *(Psalms 13)*

Like the ancient Hebrews, there are times we express our spirituality by complaining to God over our intense suffering and grief. There are also times when we affirm the presence of God, a presence that enables us to face even the most acute emotional pain. In one of his letters, the Apostle Paul described the agony that humans frequently suffer in life. He spoke of our weakness and inability to contend with circumstances, especially the inability to articulate our inner anguish and yearnings in prayer: "In the same way the Spirit also helps our weakness; for we do not know how to pray as we should, but the Spirit Himself intercedes for us with groans too deep for words" (Romans 8:26).

While maintaining spirituality involves numerous ways we discover meaning and purpose in our lives, for many it also involves using their faith. As followers of Jesus, for instance, we not only have faith, but we also live by faith. The affirmation, "the just shall live by faith," is mentioned three times in the New Testament (Romans 1:17; Galatians 3:11; Hebrews 10:38), and with the exception of a small particle in one reference all three statements are exactly the same in the Greek text ('o OE 8(Kat0<; EK nfon:(J)<; crc'tat). Faith is not optional for those desiring to follow Jesus. It is synonymous with following him. With faith we begin our journey with Jesus, and through faith we cope with life's biggest obstacles (Matthew 17:20).

Surviving loss is no exception. In managing our own grief, faith becomes a therapeutic tool. How often does the Scripture affirm that God is for us in all circumstances, actively working for our good (Romans 8:28)? How many instances does the Bible refer to a merciful God who "comforts us in our affliction" (2 Corinthians 1:3-4)? We are assured of his presence, no matter what our life situation might be:

> *For I am sure that neither death, nor life, nor angels,*
> *nor principalities,*
> *nor things present, nor things to come, nor powers, nor height,*
> *nor depth, nor anything else in all creation,*
> *will be able to separate us*
> *from the love of God in Christ Jesus our Lord.*
> (Romans 8:38-39)

The Bible acknowledges that the just shall live by faith. We should not overlook the importance of the word "live." Living is what we do each day. It involves trivial issues like shopping at the market or filling the car with gas. It includes meaningful activities like sharing an outing with family, attending a daughter's recital, or bringing flowers on an anniversary. It embraces mandatory behaviors like completing tasks at work or school. And sometimes living involves struggling with turbulent undercurrents of emotions sparked by the loss of a loved one. In those moments of loss--the cold, frightful, devastating terrible moments-we are not alone, nor are we destroyed. God is there for us: "He heals the brokenhearted and binds up their wounds" (Ps. 147:3). Through faith in him we can endure all things (Philippians 4:13).

The power of spirituality and faith in coping with significant losses is demonstrated by an experience shared by Siroj Sorajjakool, professor of religion, psychology, and counseling at Loma Linda University. In his book *When Sickness Heals: The Place of Religious Belief in Healthcare*, he writes this about his father's death:

> *"When my dad first learned that his cancer had metastasized, his theological stance was initially for God's intervention. He refused to believe otherwise. As time passed, he got worse and gradually came to see God as the One who*

offered strength and courage. However, he wanted very much to be a witness, to be cheerful and upbeat even in the face of death, and when sadness overwhelmed him, he felt disappointed with himself He wanted to sing and laugh and be courageous, but he was, at the same time, sad and frightened and depressed. On his deathbed, as friends gathered, he said: "I thought I ought to be strong. I thought I ought to smile and be cheerful. I thought I ought to be an example of faith and not let this fear affect me. I tried. I tried really hard. But I did not succeed. When I try to smile, I feel my tears. When I try to project courage, I am overwhelmed with fear. When I try to laugh, I cannot convince myself of its humor. I am afraid. I am sad. I am confused, and I learned through this entire experience that it is all right. It is all right to be afraid, to feel sad, to worry and have faith in God at the same time."

Just before he died, Siroj's dad came to fully integrate finiteness into his theological perspective. He learned that it is all right to be sad and to have faith at the same time. It is all right to be discouraged and to trust God at the same time, and to be depressed and to know that God will always remain by your side."

The use of spirituality in managing grief is similar to the grief process itself. Everyone proceeds through grief in his or her own manner, and everyone manifests spirituality in his or her own individual fashion. Some find comfort and solace in public worship, prayer, and Bible studies. Others depend more on private devotions, prayers, and meditation. Some discover strength in large or small groups. Others acquire emotional stamina from inner resources. Authentic spirituality cannot be prescribed by others. Each mourner must chart his or her own way through the painful and difficult journey of grief. Keeping in touch with your spirituality, whether it is expressed as faith or railing, is a vital part of making your way through this most excruciating of all human experiences.

Managing Grief is Aided by Openness to Those Who Care

We are told that Jesus regularly traveled through the towns and villages of Galilee, preaching the good news of the kingdom (Luke

8:1). The twelve disciples accompanied him, along with several prominent women who "ministered" to him from their resources (Luke 8:2-3). The word translated "ministered" is a verbal form of the word "deacon." Literally, these women "deaconed" him. There is also another reference about angels ministering to Jesus after his temptation experience in the wilderness (Mark 1:13). The same verb is used. The angels "deaconed" him. The point here is that even Jesus sometimes needed and received encouragement from others. If this was true for Jesus, how much more is it true for us? You and I are not sufficient in ourselves for life. We all need support from others. Although we are called to be ministers of comfort to others, we also need the ministry of comfort from others. Our ability to handle grief depends, in part, upon our openness to this gift.

The strength that comes from others became especially real for me beginning on August 28, 2004. On that day, the day of my mother's funeral, we discovered that our youngest daughter had been murdered. I cannot begin to describe the emotional implosion triggered by the words *"Dad, Kym is dead,"* a terse phone message from my son who discovered her body. And I do not have words to describe how I felt when I repeated those words to my wife before we collapsed into each other's arms, holding each other as though our world was falling apart, which it was. As never before, I realized that not one of us is truly adequate for life. We need each other.

Over the next few months my wife and I received many things from friends and neighbors, everything from baked goods to flowers, from emails to candles. We were appreciative and grateful for the generous and caring responses from so many people. But what encouraged us the most was simply the fact that people were caring; they were there for us and with us. They supported us when we struggled and hugged us when we cried. These friends "deaconed" us and that was most empowering.

In the years since our daughter's death, I have discovered that grief is a gift and that it contains hidden grace. As a gift, the ability to grieve is built into our neural wiring. We are born with the ability to respond to threatening situations with the "flight-fight-freeze" response. This response enables us to survive situations that might threaten our existence. In a similar manner, we are born with the grief response. This particular ability enables us to endure significant losses throughout our life. Both responses are "givens" in that they come with the gift of life which we all received. Since Kym's death I have increasingly become grateful for the gift to grieve because without this ability I don't think I could survive.

I have also recognized that the gift of bereavement contains hidden grace. This grace is there for all who grieve, whether an individual recognizes it or not. The grace, however, is not in the event of loss itself, whatever the loss may entail. The grace is in our response to the loss. That's because there is a nurturing power and presence that, if recognized, sustains us through the grieving process. Also, there is grace in the possibility that bereavement provides each person the opportunity to grow, to develop dimensions of one's being that were neglected before the loss.

I discovered the possibility of personal growth in my own response to Kym's death. In the immediate aftermath of that experience, I focused upon the person who took her life. I was filled with anger, resentment, and hatred. I wanted revenge and feelings of vengeance became a daily companion. In time, I realized that these thoughts and feelings were only damaging me. So, I began responding differently. Rather than focusing upon resentment for the person who took her life, I began being intentionally grateful for Kym's life. Whenever the negative feelings surfaced, I refocused my attention to Kym. I recalled experiences in her life, and qualities of her life, for which I was grateful. This was difficult at first, but practicing gratitude every day slowly began to diminish the negative emotions and it transformed me in the process.

Practicing gratitude facilitated my awakening to the grace dimension in suffering. Does the focus upon grace and other gifts hidden in suffering eradicate the pain and agony that randomly floods my soul like a wave? No. Does it diminish the lingering sadness from losing our daughter or mean we don't hurt anymore? Absolutely not. The suffering from the loss continues. However, the grace concealed in grief provides some very nurturing gifts for everyone who mourns, including the following:

- Grace encourages us to choose life again.

- Grace enables us to live with questions for which there are no answers.

- Grace allows us to release painful emotions that diminish our humanity.

- Grace enables us to bear the agony of loss in a healthier manner.

- Grace helps us understand that wounding and healing are not opposites. They are part of the same process that enables us to become more compassionate towards others who suffer.

Over the past decade, focusing upon that for which I am grateful, rather than fretting over that which is hateful and repulsive, has completely changed one dimension of my life. I am much more attuned to gratitude in daily situations than I ever was before Kym's death. For some time now, I end each day meditating upon all that I experienced that day, focusing only upon events and situations for which I am grateful. This practice continues to have a profound effect upon the quality of my life. Rather than being defined by resentment over past events or present negative experiences, I am more attuned towards gratitude. My worldview continues to be calibrated towards gratefulness and this has tremendously improved the quality of my life. This is only one obvious value of meditative spirituality.

So, how do I survive my daughter's death, one of the most profound defining moments of my life? I've been asked that question countless times since that August morning in 2004. How was I able to process those awe-full emotions and maintain my sanity? How do I now make it through each day with the memories? How will I find the strength I'll need tomorrow? My answer has been, and will always be, the same-through faith and friends. I cope with loss through the strength of faith and friends. Both are as empowering as they are therapeutic.

A significant loss can shatter us as persons. Grief, on the other hand, provides the opportunity for us to survive the loss and grow through the process. Grief nurtures wholeness when we are broken by loss... and that is grace!

Going Inside

Take a few minutes to go consider how you usually respond to significant losses.

Have you used any of the suggestions mentioned in this chapter?

What other strategies have you used to manage your grief? In what ways have you grown as a person through your bereavements?

Can you identify any hidden grace in your experiences?

What specific practices could you use to nurture your own wholeness?

"The death of someone loved changes our lives forever. And the movement from the "before" to the "after" is almost always a long, painful journey. From my own experiences with loss as well as those of the thousands of grieving people I have worked with over the years, I have learned that if we are to heal we cannot skirt the outside edges of our grief Instead, we must journey all through it, sometimes meandering the side roads. sometimes plowing directly into its raw center."

-- Alan D. Wolfelt, Ph.D.

Chapter Five

The Power of Spirituality When Life is
Broken

*"A principle of the spiritual approach to healthcare is that
while adversity befalls everyone, it is possible to grow
through it. People often become stronger emotionally, more
resilient and more mature. Indeed, such maturity is difficult
to develop without trials to undergo and obstacles to
overcome. Caring still involves the relief of unnecessary pain
and suffering where possible, but spiritual awareness can
add a powerful and much-needed dimension whenever our
human limits are reached. The spiritual approach fosters a
positive attitude even in the most heart-rending situations.
By focusing on both inner and external sources of strength,
spiritual awareness encourages calm in the place of anxiety
and hope in place of despair."*

--Dr. Larry Culliford, Royal College of Psychiatrists
in Great Britain

As I began writing this final chapter, a friend called to tell me that
his wife had been placed in Hospice care. She has been suffering
from breast cancer for two years and treatment has been ineffective.
Her time is now limited. Her husband and extended family are
crushed.

Their spirit is broken. Yet, in spite of this critical situation, they are
sustained by faith. This is the nature of spirituality. It has the power
to nurture wholeness and meaning when life is broken and senseless.
My friend's experience underlines a harsh fact: Life is fragile.

Every person is vulnerable to life's unexpected crises. It doesn't matter if the experience is the death of a loved one, a divorce, a physical or emotional illness, financial reversal, or merely the stress of tolerating a broken and empty existence. Critical events can negatively impact one's total wellbeing. Spirituality, however, enables persons to find meaning, hope, and serenity in the presence of physical and emotional distress. Numerous studies indicate that spirituality can improve coping skills, promote feelings of optimism and hope, reduce feelings of depression and anxiety, improve significant relationships, and nurture healthy behaviors. Spiritual practices can foster healing when curing is not an option. Particular spiritual practices can have a positive impact upon one's holistic health, as well as the quality of life.

Research at some of the leading medical institutions and universities affirms a positive relationship between spirituality and health. Harold G. Koenig, MD, from Duke Medical School, refers to this relationship as "the healing power of faith." Herbert Benson, MD, of Harvard Medical School, affirmed that we are "biologically wired for God". Is there an actual connection between faith and health? Does faith empower persons to cope with the stressors of daily life, such as physical and emotional illness, personal conflicts, behavioral problems, and significant losses such as death? Contemporary research reveals that faith and spirituality do indeed improve our holistic (mind-body-spirit) health, boost our sense of wellbeing, and enable us to cope with critical life events.

The Nature of Spirituality

Researchers do not always agree on the meaning of spirituality. Some describe it as a search for personal identity, to understand the "meaning of life," or to find ways of reducing suffering, getting along with others, and having a sense of inner peace" and happiness. Others define it in terms of religious practices. The definition often involves ethical or moral guidelines for behavior, beliefs about the nature of consciousness, and life after death, as well as clues about improving the quality of life. Yet, however the concept is defined, the nature of spirituality includes the following features:

• Spirituality is not the same as religion although it can have religious expressions.

• Spirituality embraces creativity, transcendence, a sense of wonder, ecstasy, mystery, and awe.

• Spirituality welcomes a sense of, and relationship with, the Divine.

• Spirituality involves experiencing a deep-seated sense of meaning and purpose in life, together with a sense of belonging. It is about acceptance, integration and wholeness.

• Because it includes a sense of meaning and purpose, spirituality is especially energized in times of emotional stress, physical and mental illness, loss, and death. These experiences both threaten and destabilize our sense of wholeness and well-being.

• Spirituality embraces several skills that enable us to integrate the various dimensions of our experience, maintain wholeness, and cope more effectively with life in the process. These skills include, but are not limited to, the following: (1) Religious practices like worship, prayer, reading scripture, and daily devotions; (2) Meditation and mindfulness; (3) Creative activities such as painting, sculpture, and music; (4) Contemplative activities such as poetry, journaling, and reflective reading;(5) Involvement in charitable organizations; (6) Regular/daily caring behaviors such as gratitude, kindness, and forgiveness; (7) Quality experiences with family and friends.

The Creative and Healing Power of Spirituality

In the past several decades many areas of healthcare have begun to recover the spiritual sources that historically have been associated with healing practices. The effect of spirituality on holistic health is now an area of continuous research. This is an area of interest at the National Institutes of Health and organizations related to the NIH.

Currently, most medical schools in the United States offer courses on spirituality and health. Agencies such as the John Templeton Foundation support the development of programs on spirituality and health in medical schools and residency training programs. Also, several prominent medical schools and universities have institutes on spirituality and health that are designed to study the impact of spirituality and religion on holistic health, as well as in the development of new spiritual techniques that have a positive influence on health and daily coping. This research is showing that spirituality offers numerous positive benefits for addressing everyday critical events that have a defining impact upon human development and well-being. Some of the more prominent benefits are noted here.

Spirituality can have a positive effect on physical health. Research indicates that spiritual practices can contribute to healing and a sense of well-being. Improving your spiritual health might not cure an illness, but it may help you feel better, prevent some health problems, and enable you to cope with illness, stress, or even death. One of the leaders in the spirituality-health field of research is Harold G. Koenig, M.D., an Associate Professor of Psychiatry and Behavioral Sciences and Assistant Professor of Medicine at Duke University Medical Center. Koenig has published widely in both books and professional journals. Two of his books, *The Healing Power of Faith: Science Explores Medicine's Last Great Frontier* and *Is Religion Good for Your Health?* contain numerous examples of how spirituality and religion influence positive medical outcomes. Some of the research results include:

- People who attend church regularly are hospitalized much less often than people who never or rarely participate in religious services.

- People who attend religious services regularly have stronger immune systems than their less religious counterparts. It was found that people who went to church regularly had significantly lower blood levels of interleukin-6 (IL-6), which rises with unrelieved chronic stress. High levels of IL-6 reflect a weakened immune system, which, in turn, increases the risk of infection, autoimmune disease, and certain cancers.

• A growing body of research shows that religious people are both physically healthier into later life and live longer than nonreligious persons. Religious faith appears to protect the elderly from the two major afflictions of later life, cardiovascular disease and cancer. In this regard, religion may be as significant a protective factor as not smoking in terms of survival and longevity.

> • The Journal of the American Heart Association (March 2000) reported a study that shows meditation can reduce the risk of cardiovascular disease.

> • Of 300 studies on spirituality in scientific journals, the National Institute of Healthcare Research discovered that three-fourths revealed that religion had a positive effect on health.

> • Dean Ornish, M.D., in *Love and Survival: The Scientific Basis for the Healing Power of Intimacy*, explores the scientific evidence that love, intimacy, and relationships directly affects our health and survival. Consider these questions: Do you have anyone who really cares for you? Who feels close to you? Who loves you? Who wants to help you? In whom you confide? Persons who answer no to these questions, may have three to five times higher risk of premature death and disease from all causes.

These are merely a few examples of how spirituality can positively impact one's physical health. Current research, in larger numbers, continues to validate and expand these types of results.

Spirituality nurtures emotional, social, and cognitive health. Spirituality also has a positive effect upon other dimensions of personhood, especially the cognitive, emotional, and social dimensions. Results from many of the medical and psychological studies can be found in resources such as Harold Koenig, MD, *The Link Between Religion and Health: Psychoneuroimmunology and the Faith Factor*; Andrew Newberg, MD, *How God Changes Your Brain*; and Koenig, McCullough, & Larson, *Handbook of Religion and Health*. The following are a few examples.

• Persons who attend worship services more than once a week have half the risk of major depression as those who attend less often. Also, people with major depression who believe in a caring higher being are also 75% more likely to get relief from medication.

• Regular prayer increases your concern for other people, creating positive sense of connection that could help you make your world a brighter, better place.

• Focusing on your spiritual values can quiet the anterior cingulate cortex that fires when things start going wrong in your life, raising your stress levels.

• Singing together, such as in religious services, increases oxytocin which, in turn, strengthens a sense of community, caring, and bonding.

• Thinking about God or other spiritual beliefs keeps you calm under fire, which may explain why deeply spiritual people tend to live longer, healthier, and happier lives.

Spirituality enhances our coping ability. Patients who are spiritual frequently use their beliefs in coping with illness, pain, and stressful life events, such as the death of a loved one. Some studies indicate that those who are spiritual tend to have a more positive outlook, a better quality of life, and cope more effectively with life. Christina M. Puchalski, MD, from The George Washington University Medical Center Departments of Medicine and Health Care Sciences, reports on several studies in a paper entitled *The Role of Spirituality in Health Care:*

> • Studies indicate that those who are spiritual tend to have a more positive outlook and a better quality of life. For example, patients with advanced cancer who found comfort from their religious and spiritual beliefs were more satisfied with their lives, were happier, and had less pain.

> • Spirituality is an essential part of the "existential domain" measured in quality-of-life scores. Positive reports on those

measures-a meaningful personal existence, fulfillment of life goals, and a feeling that life to that point had been worthwhile-correlated with a good quality of life for patients with advanced disease.

• Some studies have also looked at the role of spirituality regarding pain. One study showed that spiritual well-being was related to the ability to enjoy life even in the midst of symptoms, including pain.

• Spiritual beliefs can help patients cope with disease and face death. When asked what helped them cope with their gynecologic cancer, 93% of 108 women cited spiritual beliefs. In addition, 75% of these patients stated that religion had a significant place in their lives, and 49% said they had become more spiritual after their diagnosis.

• Regarding bereavement, a study of 145 parents whose children had died of cancer found that 80% received comfort from their religious beliefs 1 year after their child's death. Those parents had better physiologic and emotional adjustment. In addition, 40% of those parents reported a strengthening of their own religious commitment over the course of the year prior to their child's death.

Spirituality facilitates healing even when curing is not possible. These two words, healing and curing, are often used interchangeably, but they can have very different meanings. Curing has to do with the removal of all signs and symptoms of a physical or mental illness.

A person is cured when the disorder is finished and there are no symptoms left. Healing involves something much deeper, personal, and existential. It involves the harmonious alignment of the physical, emotional, mental and spiritual aspects of our being and how we relate to the world. The result is a greater experience of wholeness, wellness and soundness. Healing is a process of rebuilding our life anew from chaos and disorder; it is about becoming whole. In this regard, a person may be cured, but not healed; or healed but not cured. The distinction between healing and curing is important for addressing bereavement. Significant losses often break and shatter the human spirit. Spiritual practices, like the ones mentioned above, nurture wholeness and healing.

Spirituality enables us to recreate our worldview to produce a new sense of meaning when our emotional wellbeing is shattered. When we experience significant losses our personal world has to be re- configured. Years ago when my Dad was slowly dying of cancer I recall telling him how difficult it would be for me to restructure my life (world) without him in it. That was a challenging process, but spirituality enabled me to do just that. Each member of our family, in his or her own way, had to repeat the re-configuring process on the occasion of my daughter's death. A few months after that tragic loss, I received the following email from my son who lives in Denver. His email describing a "dancing napkin" is one example of how spirituality was enabling him to re-configure his own worldview which was shattered by his sister's death.

> *Dad,*
>
>> *You know that since Kym's death, I've struggled with the issues of mind/body/spirit/soul and "what are those entities?", and "what happens to those when we die?" And that was a depressing subject, because in my mind, I thought everything that it means to "be alive" is wrapped up in the coordinated workings of the cells in the human body. I thought it was all there, mind, consciousness, etc. I thought it was all just a by-product of being alive. What's this soul/spirit thing and how could it NOT be a part of just being a living body with wants and desires, likes and dislikes? My thinking up until this point was that the soul and spirit died with the body, with death just being a form of non-existence.*
>>
>> *But today something happened that changed that perspective for me. I was taking a break from work and was hanging out outside enjoying a beautiful Colorado fall day, complete with a cool and substantial breeze. Then out of the corner of my eye, I notice a paper napkin that looked like it was dancing on the grass. As the breeze blew it, it looked alive, even playful, even though I knew it wasn't alive. And then*

all of a sudden it started making its way toward me in a very playful way...its actions sort of reminded me of a puppy wanting me to play with it. AND THEN IT HIT ME! It was the wind making the napkin appear to be alive, it wasn't the physical make-up of the napkin which gave it "life" (or the appearance of life). It was the breeze! With the wind not blowing on the napkin, the napkin was dead, lifeless. And even though I could still feel the breeze on my face, it wasn't affecting the napkin anymore. So this experience made me realize how the spirit/body thing could intertwine together for a beautiful life experience. And I can also see how the spirit could live on without the body. Like the wind. it's the spirit that gives the body its personality that makes the napkin dance. But without the spirit, the body is like a napkin with no wind. And like the wind, the spirit doesn't die just because it's not interacting with the body anymore.

Anyway, hope that wasn't too much "babble". Through all this I'm just looking/ or new perspectives on life. And that "dancing napkin" was very helpful to me and gave me a new perspective on how spirit and body might interact. But in the very least, it got me to realize that just because something appears to be alive, doesn't mean that the physical make-up of that object explains the "life" we see in that object. That may come from non-body things like spirit (and wind).

Art

The take-away truth here is that there is no life without death, pleasure without pain, health without sickness, security without insecurity, well-being without suffering, and certainty without loss. The problem is that we are notorious for wanting to exclude death, pain, sickness, suffering, insecurity, and loss from our experience. Spiritual skills enable us to integrate our life when it is shattered by human experiences. In brief, when life falls apart spirituality is healing, and the gift of hidden grace can make one whole.

Closing Thoughts

As you finish processing this material in grief and bereavement, I hope you have found the material to be helpful, informative, and encouraging. My wish is that the content will provide some effective resources for your own responses to losses throughout your life, as well as enabling you to be an effective caretaker, either as a professional or merely as a caring friend, to others who are grieving.

In closing, I would like to highlight several observations that are effective in understanding the nature of grief and nurturing a healthful response to grief.

- A strong support group cannot be over-emphasized. Contemporary research in neuroscience is reaffirming the importance of personal attachments. From birth throughout life, connections to, and experiences with, significant others influences our brain, which in turn regulates our moods, thoughts, desires, memories, and behaviors. Healthy social relationships are vital for the wholesome processing of grief.

- Spirituality is proven to be crucial in processing grief. Practicing spiritual skills are very nurturing in coping with significant losses and growing as a person in that process.

- The healing aspect of grief should be a primary focus throughout bereavement. Although grieving is not a pleasant or easy task, it is a healing process that impacts our total being.

- There are many ways to understand and make sense out of grief. It is not as simple as any of the grief sequence (stage) models make it appear. Grief takes many forms since persons grieve in their own way, experiences that are shaped by numerous variables.

- Quantum physics offers one analogy that can be used to understand grief. A photon, for example, can be viewed as a particle or as a wave. It is both particle and wave, but not at the same time. It's what it is perceived to be when it is observed. In a similar fashion, some persons perceive grief as a process of stages. Others experience it as a wave that comes at various times with different intensity. And some persons do not perceive it as either a stage or a wave. Grief is a highly personal and individual experience. All of the perceptions to identify grief can be true or not true. That's the nature of grief. It cannot easily be defined, but it is experienced by everyone.

• Grief can be approached and managed in healthy or unhealthy ways. This also is individual (what helps one may hinder another), but care and attention are priorities in coping with this experience.

Grief is universally recognized as a response to any significant loss, especially the death of a loved one. It is important to differentiate between the loss (death) itself and the grief process that follows. The two are related but are not the same. The death of a loved one is a disturbing event that can shatter our world, destabilize our emotional balance, diminish our sense of wellbeing, and flood our life with various painful and sorrowful emotions. Grief, on the other hand, is an innate holistic response to the loss, enabling us to cope with the normal flood of intense emotions associated with the death and sustain us as we reconfigure our life without the presence of the loved one. Since we are born with the ability to grieve, the process is a natural gift.

Grief as an instinctive gift also provides the opportunity to transform particular aspects of our life. We can grow into a more wholesome person, as we nurture embryonic qualities of our individual self. Depending upon how we process the grief and respond to the loss, we can become more caring, generous, considerate, thankful, forgiving, or stronger. We can completely change the way we live each day. There are countless ways each of us can develop our individual potential. This possibility of becoming a better (whole) person through adversity is grace, a quality which is often obscured by the emotional intensity of the loss. This is why it is labeled "hidden" grace. It is inherent in all forms of grief and is available to all, regardless of who experiences the loss or how deserving the person might be. That is the nature of grace. To more fully understand bereavement as a holistic event, this possibility of personal growth, rather than final resolution of grief, should be a primary focus.

As long as you live, may you discover the grace embedded in all your losses. Those losses will not be easy or pleasant, but there is grace to sustain you and nurture you as you redefine yourself and reconfigure your life. And that is the gift!

Going Inside

Based upon the ideas about spirituality presented in this chapter, give some thought to these questions:

Do you consider yourself to be a spiritual person?

Given its complex nature, what aspects of spirituality are dominant in your life?

In times of difficulty, what spiritual practices have been most helpful for you?

What spiritual practices might you consider practicing?

How might your life be different if you were more spiritual?

What spiritual practices have been helpful in growing through loss and grief?

All healing is first spiritual healing, from radiation therapy
to antidepressant medication.
Healing the spirit is necessary to heal the body.
Treatment fails when we do not do this.
We cannot cut the flesh without addressing the soul.
The soul must give its permission.
It must allow physical manipulation, surgery, and drugs to succeed.
Its help furthers our therapies.
Its resistance weakens our efforts, makes our antibiotics ineffective,
and prevents surgical incisions from healing.

--Lewis Mehl-Madrona, M.D., Ph.D.

Additional Resources

In addition to the sources mentioned in the text, the author has found these additional resources to be very helpful in understanding grief and bereavement in human experience.

Carolyn DeArmond Blevins, *A Journey of Peace and Pain: Learning From Loss*

Herbert Benson, MD, *Timeless Healing*

Kathleen Brehony, *The Darkest Hour: How Suffering Begins the Journey to Wisdom*

Coping with Grief and Loss: A Guide to Healing (Harvard Medical School Special Report)

David E. Crutchley & Gerald L. Borchert, Editors, *Assaulted by Grief: Finding God in the Broken Places*

Louis Cozolino, *The Neuroscience of Psychotherapy: Building and Rebuilding the Human Brain*

Larry Gulliford, *The Psychology of Spirituality*

Harold G. Koenig & George W. Bowman, *Dying, Grieving, Faith, and Family: A Pastoral Care Approach*

Harold Koenig, MD, *The Link Between Religion and Health: Psychoneuroimmunology and the Faith Factor*

Harold Koenig MD, Michael McCullough MD, & David Larson MD, *Handbook of Religion and Health*

Harold Koenig, MD, *Medicine, Religion, and Health: Where Science and Spirituality Meet*

Coval B. MacDonald, "Loss and Bereavement," in *Clinical Handbook of Pastoral Counseling*, edited by Robert J. Wicks, Richard D. Parsons, and Donald E. Capps

Elizabeth Levang & Sherokee Ilse, *Remembering With Love*

Jeff Levine, *God, Faith, and Health*

Mitchell, K & Anderson, H., *All Our Losses, All Our Griefs: Resources for Pastoral Care*

Andrew Newberg, MD, and Mark Robert Waldman, *How God Changes Your Brain: Breakthrough Findings from a Leading Neuroscientist*

Henri J.M. Nouwen, *The Wounded Healer: Ministry in Contemporary Society*

Wayne Oates, *Anxiety in Christian Experience*

Randall O'Brien, *Set Free by Forgiveness: The Way to Peace and Healing*

Dean Ornish, MD, *Love and Survival*

Ashley Davis Prend, *Transcending Loss*

Lewis Smedes, *The Art of Forgiving*

Philip Yancey, *Where Is God When It Hurts?*

Philip Yancey, *What's So Amazing About Grace?*